Ladies' Home Journal®

100 GREAT APPETIZER AND SNACK RECIPES

LADIES' HOME JOURNAL™ BOOKS
New York / Des Moines

LADIES' HOME JOURNAL™ BOOKS
An Imprint of Meredith® Books

100 GREAT APPETIZER AND SNACK RECIPES
Editor: Shelli McConnell
Writer/Researcher: Carol Prager
Copy Editor: Jennifer Miller
Associate Art Director: Tom Wegner
Food Stylist: William Smith
Prop Stylist: Betty Alfenito
Photographer: Steven Mark Needham
Electronic Production Coordinator: Paula Forest
Production Manager: Douglas Johnston

Vice President and Editorial Director: Elizabeth P. Rice
Executive Editor: Kay M. Sanders
Art Director: Ernest Shelton
Managing Editor: Christopher Cavanaugh

President, Book Group: Joseph J. Ward
Vice President, Retail Marketing: Jamie L. Martin
Vice President, Direct Marketing: Timothy Jarrell

LADIES' HOME JOURNAL®
Publishing Director and Editor-in-Chief: Myrna Blyth
Food Editor: Jan Turner Hazard
Associate Food Editors: Susan Sarao Westmoreland, Lisa Brainerd

On the cover: Zucchini Ribbons, page 141

Meredith Corporation
Chairman of the Executive Committee: E.T. Meredith III
Chairman of the Board and Chief Executive Officer: Jack D. Rehm
President and Chief Operating Officer: William T. Kerr

All of us at Ladies' Home Journal Books are dedicated to providing you with the ideas and recipe information you need to create wonderful foods. We guarantee your satisfaction with this book for as long as you own it. We welcome your comments and suggestions. Please write to us at: Ladies' Home Journal Books, RW 240, 1716 Locust Street, Des Moines, IA 50309-3023.

To ensure that Ladies' Home Journal recipes meet the highest standards for flavor, nutrition, appearance and reliability, we test them a minimum of three times in our Test Kitchen. That makes for quality you can count on.

If you would like to order additional copies of any of our books, call 1-800-678-2803 or check with your local bookstore.

Anytime Appetizers

When you want to excite the taste buds and
jump start a meal, it's time to create an appetizer
or snack. At Ladies' Home Journal ®,
we selected our all-time favorite appetizer
recipes to bring to you in this astounding
assortment of spreadable dips, party-style finger
foods, elegant hors d'oeuvres, Italian antipasto,
and nibbles from the bar. Guaranteed, select any
of these fixin's and your next feast for friends or
family will be off to the perfect start.

CONTENTS

The Big Dipper

Fast and fresh dips—the perfect match for crudités, crackers, and chips.

6

Glorious Antipasto

A hearty selection of Italian favorites.

32

Bites from the Bar

An assortment of nibblers served at restaurants and bars.

56

Perfect Party Food

Pass the platter or create a bountiful buffet. Either way, these appetizers will be the star of your show.

82

Easy and Elegant Starters

Ultimate fare for a sit-down occasion.

118

Index

142

THE BIG

DIPPER

A dip is one of the easiest appetizers to make. Hot or cold, smooth or with a touch of crunch, dips are fast, fresh, and fabulous tasting. Classics that are perfect with crudités include Fresh Spinach Dip, Creamy Blue Cheese Dip, and Herbed Yogurt Cheese Dip. Dip a tortilla chip in Classic Salsa Cruda and Salsa Verde. And chips, pita wedges, crackers, and veggies can all take a dip in a bowl of Grilled Eggplant Dip or Double Tomato Jam. So if you're ready, start dipping!

ASPARAGUS WITH TARRAGON DIPPING SAUCE

This dip says spring. We like slender asparagus stalks no more than ½ inch in diameter. If your stalks are larger, adjust the cooking time.

Prep time: 10 minutes
Cooking time: 2 minutes
Degree of difficulty: easy

3 **pounds thin asparagus, cut into 5-inch spears**
½ **cup mayonnaise**
¼ **cup sour cream**
2 **tablespoons minced shallots**
2 **tablespoons chopped fresh tarragon**
1 **teaspoon fresh lemon juice**
¼ **teaspoon salt**
¼ **teaspoon freshly ground pepper**
   Pinch ground red pepper

1 Bring 4 quarts of salted water to a boil in a large pot. Add the asparagus, return to a boil, and cook about 2 minutes or until just tender. Rinse and drain under cold running water. Pat asparagus dry with paper towels. (Can be made ahead. Wrap and refrigerate up to 24 hours.)

2 For tarragon sauce, combine the mayonnaise, sour cream, shallots, tarragon, lemon juice, salt, freshly ground pepper, and red pepper in a small bowl until well mixed. (Can be made ahead. Cover and refrigerate up to 24 hours.)

3 Arrange asparagus on a platter and serve with tarragon sauce. Makes 20 servings.

PER SERVING WITH 1 TEASPOON SAUCE		DAILY GOAL
Calories	40	2,000 (F), 2,500 (M)
Total fat	3 g	60 g or less (F), 70 g or less (M)
Saturated fat	1 g	20 g or less (F), 23 g or less (M)
Cholesterol	2 mg	300 mg or less
Sodium	33 mg	2,400 mg or less
Carbohydrates	0 g	250 g or more
Protein	0 g	55 g to 90 g

NOTES

FRESH SPINACH DIP

We've lightened up this classic dip with fresh spinach and reduced-fat sour cream. To make this appetizer a beta carotene bonanza, serve it with carrot sticks and broccoli florets.

▼ *Low-fat*
▽ *Low-calorie*
  Prep time: 10 minutes
○ *Degree of difficulty: easy*

  2 cups packed fresh spinach leaves
  ½ cup reduced-fat sour cream
  ½ teaspoon salt
    Pinch ground red pepper
  ¼ cup finely chopped green onions

Combine the spinach, sour cream, salt, and red pepper in a food processor and process until smooth. Transfer to a bowl and stir in green onions. Makes 1 cup.

PER TABLESPOON		DAILY GOAL
Calories	15	2,000 (F), 2,500 (M)
Total fat	1 g	60 g or less (F), 70 g or less (M)
Saturated fat	0 g	20 g or less (F), 23 g or less (M)
Cholesterol	3 mg	300 mg or less
Sodium	77 mg	2,400 mg or less
Carbohydrates	1 g	250 g or more
Protein	1 g	55 g to 90 g

CRUDITÉS WITH CLASS

• If you prepare crudités in advance, refresh the cut vegetables in ice water before storing. Drain well, then seal them in plastic bags lined with a paper towel to absorb excess moisture.

• Multicolored crudités that are artfully arranged look wonderful in a basket around a bowl of dip.

• For large gatherings, crudités can be arranged on platters up to 2 hours in advance. Cover them with damp paper towels and mist them occasionally to remoisten.

GARDEN PARTY DIP

It tastes rich and creamy, but this dip is made with reduced-fat sour cream and yogurt. Folding the remaining sour cream in at the end helps keep the dip thick. *Also pictured on page 6.*

▽ *Low-calorie*
   Prep time: 15 minutes
○ *Degree of difficulty: easy*

- 1 **container (16 ounces) reduced-fat sour cream, divided**
- ½ **cup plain low-fat yogurt**
- 1 **cup firmly packed flat-leaf parsley**
- 2 **green onions, sliced**
- 2 **tablespoons fresh tarragon leaves**
- 1 **teaspoon anchovy paste**
- ¾ **teaspoon salt**
- ¼ **teaspoon freshly ground pepper**
  Assorted fresh vegetables (asparagus, broccoli, carrots, cherry tomatoes, cucumbers, endive, mushrooms, radishes, snowpeas)

In a blender, combine ½ cup of the sour cream, the yogurt, parsley, green onions, tarragon, anchovy paste, salt, and pepper and blend until smooth. Transfer to a medium bowl and stir in the remaining sour cream. (Can be made ahead. Cover and refrigerate up to 24 hours.) Serve with vegetables. Makes 2¼ cups.

PER TABLESPOON		DAILY GOAL
Calories	25	2,000 (F), 2,500 (M)
Total fat	2 g	60 g or less (F), 70 g or less (M)
Saturated fat	1 g	20 g or less (F), 23 g or less (M)
Cholesterol	4 mg	300 mg or less
Sodium	55 mg	2,400 mg or less
Carbohydrates	1 g	250 g or more
Protein	1 g	55 g to 90 g

NOTES

CREAMY BLUE CHEESE DIP

This easy dip is a great way to use your favorite blue cheese—imported Gorgonzola, Danish, or Stilton, or any domestic variety. We find the easiest way to mash the garlic is to use the flat side of a chef's knife.

Prep time: 10 minutes plus chilling
O *Degree of difficulty: easy*

1 **package (8 ounces) cream cheese, softened**
4 **ounces blue cheese, crumbled (1 cup)**
2 **tablespoons butter, softened (no substitutions)**
¼ **cup sour cream**
1 **small garlic clove, mashed to a paste**
2 **tablespoons heavy *or* whipping cream**

Combine the cream cheese, blue cheese, butter, sour cream, and garlic in a food processor and process until smooth. With machine on, pour in the cream and blend well. Transfer to a serving bowl and cover with plastic wrap. Refrigerate at least 2 hours or overnight. (Can be made ahead. Cover and refrigerate up to 2 days.) Makes 2 cups.

PER TABLESPOON		DAILY GOAL
Calories	50	2,000 (F), 2,500 (M)
Total fat	5 g	60 g or less (F), 70 g or less (M)
Saturated fat	3 g	20 g or less (F), 23 g or less (M)
Cholesterol	14 mg	300 mg or less
Sodium	79 mg	2,400 mg or less
Carbohydrates	0 g	250 g or more
Protein	1 g	55 g to 90 g

NOTES

HERBED YOGURT CHEESE DIP

We also love this dip served on top of baked potatoes.

▼ *Low-fat*
▽ *Low-calorie*
  Prep time: 10 minutes plus standing
○ *Degree of difficulty: easy*

4	**cups plain nonfat *or* low-fat yogurt**
2	**tablespoons minced green onion**
2	**tablespoons chopped fresh parsley**
2	**tablespoons chopped fresh basil**
½	**teaspoon minced garlic**
	Assorted fresh vegetables

1 Place nonfat or low-fat yogurt in a colander lined with layers of cheesecloth or a clean kitchen towel, then set colander over a large bowl. Cover and refrigerate 3 hours for nonfat yogurt or 5 hours for low-fat yogurt.

2 Transfer the strained yogurt cheese into a medium bowl and discard the liquid. Stir together the yogurt cheese, the green onion, parsley, basil, and garlic. Serve with assorted fresh vegetables. Makes 2 cups.

PER TABLESPOON		DAILY GOAL
Calories	10	2,000 (F), 2,500 (M)
Total Fat	0 g	60 g or less (F), 70 g or less (M)
Saturated fat	0 g	20 g or less (F), 23 g or less (M)
Cholesterol	0 mg	300 mg or less
Sodium	10 mg	2,400 mg or less
Carbohydrates	1 g	250 g or more
Protein	1 g	55 g to 90 g

DOUBLE TOMATO JAM

Two kinds of tomatoes—fresh and dried—are cooked together in this colorful spread, perfect served with our homemade Garlic Toasts.

▽ *Low-calorie*
  Prep time: 20 minutes plus cooling
  Cooking time: 25 to 30 minutes
O *Degree of difficulty: easy*

12 **plum tomatoes (about 2 pounds)**
¼ **cup (½ ounce) chopped sun-dried tomatoes**
½ **cup boiling water**
2 **tablespoons extra-virgin olive oil**
1 **cup thinly sliced shallots**
2 **teaspoons minced garlic**
2 **teaspoons grated fresh ginger**
2 **tablespoons balsamic vinegar**
1 **tablespoon packed brown sugar**
½ **teaspoon salt**
¼ **teaspoon freshly ground pepper**
  Garlic Toasts (recipe, page 31) *or* **assorted crackers**

1 Prepare grill or preheat broiler. Grill the plum tomatoes 3 inches from heat source, turning occasionally, about 2 minutes per side or until skin is blackened. Cool slightly and chop coarsely.

2 Combine the sun-dried tomatoes and boiling water in a small bowl and let stand 5 minutes. Meanwhile, heat the oil in a large skillet over medium-high heat. Add the shallots and cook about 2 minutes or until golden. Stir in the garlic and ginger and cook 30 seconds. Carefully add the plum and sun-dried tomatoes with their liquid. Cook, stirring occasionally, for 20 to 25 minutes or until mixture is thickened and most of the liquid is evaporated. Add the vinegar, sugar, salt, and pepper and cook 1 minute more. Transfer to a medium bowl and cool. (Can be made ahead. Cover and refrigerate up to 3 days.) Serve with Garlic Toasts or crackers. Makes 3 cups.

PER TABLESPOON		DAILY GOAL
Calories	15	2,000 (F), 2,500 (M)
Total fat	1 g	60 g or less (F), 70 g or less (M)
Saturated fat	0 g	20 g or less (F), 23 g or less (M)
Cholesterol	0 mg	300 mg or less
Sodium	25 mg	2,400 mg or less
Carbohydrates	2 g	250 g or more
Protein	0 g	55 g to 90 g

NOTES

ROQUEFORT-WALNUT DIP

The base for this dip is a rich and creamy cheese prepared with plain yogurt.

Prep time: 10 minutes plus standing
Degree of difficulty: easy

4 **cups plain nonfat** *or* **low-fat yogurt**
1 **cup chopped walnuts**
⅔ **cup crumbled Roquefort cheese**
Assorted fresh vegetables

1 Place the yogurt in a colander lined with layers of cheesecloth or a clean kitchen towel, then set colander over a large bowl. Cover and refrigerate 3 hours for nonfat yogurt or 5 hours for low-fat yogurt.

2 Transfer strained yogurt cheese into a medium bowl and discard liquid. Stir together the yogurt cheese, the nuts, and the Roquefort. Serve with assorted fresh vegetables. Makes 2⅔ cups.

PER TABLESPOON		DAILY GOAL
Calories	35	2,000 (F), 2,500 (M)
Total fat	2 g	60 g or less (F), 70 g or less (M)
Saturated fat	1 g	20 g or less (F), 23 g or less (M)
Cholesterol	2 mg	300 mg or less
Sodium	46 mg	2,400 mg or less
Carbohydrates	1 g	250 g or more
Protein	2 g	55 g to 90 g

NOTES

GRILLED EGGPLANT DIP

For sweet-tasting grilled eggplant, we studded it with garlic before roasting it.

▼ *Low-fat*
▽ *Low-calorie*
   Prep time: 20 minutes
   Grilling time: 35 to 45 minutes
○ *Degree of difficulty: easy*

2 **medium eggplants**
      (1¼ pounds each)
2 **garlic cloves, very thinly sliced**
1 **medium tomato**
¼ **cup chopped flat-leaf parsley**
2 **tablespoons extra-virgin olive oil**
1 **teaspoon fresh lemon juice**
¾ **teaspoon salt**
¼ **teaspoon freshly ground pepper**
¼ **cup chopped toasted walnuts**
      Assorted fresh vegetables
      Toasted French bread *or* pita bread

1 Prepare grill. Cut slits all over the eggplant with a small, sharp knife and insert the garlic into slits. Grill eggplant over medium-hot coals, turning occasionally, for 35 to 45 minutes or until charred and beginning to collapse. Meanwhile, grill the tomato, turning occasionally, for 3 to 5 minute or until beginning to char.

2 Remove skin from eggplant and discard, then cut in half lengthwise and remove as many seeds as possible. Chop eggplant and transfer to a medium bowl.

3 Peel, seed, and coarsely chop the tomato and add to the bowl. Stir in the parsley, oil, lemon juice, salt, and pepper. (Can be made ahead. Cover and refrigerate up to 8 hours.) Just before serving, stir in the walnuts. Serve with fresh vegetables and toasted bread. Makes 2 cups.

PER TABLESPOON		DAILY GOAL
Calories	25	2,000 (F), 2,500 (M)
Total fat	1 g	60 g or less (F), 70 g or less (M)
Saturated fat	0 g	20 g or less (F), 23 g or less (M)
Cholesterol	0 mg	300 mg or less
Sodium	53 mg	2,400 mg or less
Carbohydrates	3 g	250 g or more
Protein	1 g	55 g to 90 g

TARAMASALATA

This specialty appetizer from Greece features tarama, a pale orange cod roe that gives the dip a wonderful vibrant hue. Serve with pita wedges, crackers, or assorted crudités.

Prep time: 15 minutes
Cooking time: 10 minutes
○ *Degree of difficulty: easy*

1   **medium baking potato (8 ounces), peeled and cut into 1-inch chunks**
1   **package (3 ounces) cream cheese, softened**
⅓   **cup tarama (salted cod, carp, *or* mullet roe) *or* 1 jar (2 ounces) red lumpfish caviar**
¼   **cup ground blanched almonds**
¼   **cup fresh lemon juice**
1   **tablespoon minced red onion**
½   **cup olive oil**
    Pita wedges *or* Garlic Pita Chips (recipe, page 31)

1 Combine the potato chunks and cold water to cover in a small saucepan; bring to a boil. Reduce heat and cook about 15 minutes or until very tender. Drain potatoes then transfer to a food mill or potato ricer. Force potatoes through the mill into a large mixing bowl.

2 Beat potatoes at high speed with the cream cheese, tarama, almonds, lemon juice, and onion until smooth. With mixer at low speed, gradually drizzle in the olive oil, beating constantly, until mixture is very smooth. Serve with pita wedges or Garlic Pita Chips. Makes 2 cups.

PER TABLESPOON		DAILY GOAL
Calories	55	2,000 (F), 2,500 (M)
Total fat	5 g	60 g or less (F), 70 g or less (M)
Saturated fat	1 g	20 g or less (F), 23 g or less (M)
Cholesterol	13 mg	300 mg or less
Sodium	34 mg	2,400 mg or less
Carbohydrates	2 g	250 g or more
Protein	1 g	55 g to 90 g

NOTES

SKORDALIA

Here's a dip from Greece that can be prepared with day old bread, beans, or, as in this version, with mashed potatoes. Whatever the variation, it always includes plenty of garlic!

Prep time: 20 minutes
Cooking time: 15 minutes
O *Degree of difficulty: easy*

 1 **pound baking potatoes, peeled and cut into 1-inch chunks**
 4 **teaspoons minced garlic**
 1 **teaspoon salt**
 ¼ **cup fresh lemon juice**
 ½ **cup olive oil**
    Pita wedges

1 Combine the potatoes and cold water to cover in a medium saucepan; bring to a boil. Reduce heat and cook about 15 minutes or until very tender. Drain potatoes then transfer to a food mill or potato ricer. Force potatoes through the mill into a large mixing bowl.

2 Meanwhile, mash the garlic with the salt with the flat side of a large knife to form a paste.

3 Beat potatoes at high speed with lemon juice until smooth. With mixer at low speed, gradually drizzle in olive oil, beating constantly, until mixture is very smooth. Beat in garlic paste until blended. Serve with pita wedges. Makes 2¼ cups.

PER TABLESPOON		DAILY GOAL	
Calories	35	2,000 (F), 2,500 (M)	
Total fat	3 g	60 g or less (F), 70 g or less (M)	
Saturated fat	0 g	20 g or less (F), 23 g or less (M)	
Cholesterol	0 mg	300 mg or less	
Sodium	61 mg	2,400 mg or less	
Carbohydrates	2 g	250 g or more	
Protein	0 g	55 g to 90 g	

19

CRUNCHY JICAMA SALSA

For maximum crunch, dice each ingredient as small as possible. Be sure to have plenty of tortilla chips for dipping.

▼ *Low-fat*
▽ *Low-calorie*
   Prep time: 30 minutes
○ *Degree of difficulty: easy*

2 **cups finely diced jicama**
1 **large yellow *or* red tomato, seeded and finely diced**
½ **cup finely diced yellow pepper**
½ **cup peeled, seeded, and finely diced cucumber**
½ **cup finely diced red onion**
¼ **cup finely diced carrot**
2 **tablespoons chopped fresh cilantro**
2 **tablespoons fresh lime juice**
1 **teaspoon minced jalapeño *or* serrano chile**
¼ **teaspoon salt**
   Oven-Baked Tortilla Chips (recipe, page 31)

Combine the jicama, tomato, pepper, cucumber, onion, carrot, cilantro, lime juice, jalapeño, and salt in a large bowl. Serve with Oven-Baked Tortilla Chips. Makes 4 cups.

PER 1/4 CUP		DAILY GOAL
Calories	15	2,000 (F), 2,500 (M)
Total fat	0 g	60 g or less (F), 70 g or less (M)
Saturated fat	0 g	20 g or less (F), 23 g or less (M)
Cholesterol	0 mg	300 mg or less
Sodium	37 mg	2,400 mg or less
Carbohydrates	3 g	250 g or more
Protein	0 g	55 g to 90 g

NOTES

VEGGIES THAT TAKE THE PLUNGE

It's easy to dress veggie dippers up by using our guide for a beautiful assortment of crudités. Here's how to select, cut, and cook them.

Asparagus: Look for firm spears, ½ inch thick, and at least two-thirds green. Trim any white, woody bases. For larger spears, we recommend peeling the bottom portion of the stalk with a vegetable peeler. Blanch asparagus in a large pot of rapidly boiling salted water for 2 to 3 minutes, depending on its thickness. Immediately place the pot under cold running water. When the water is cold, transfer asparagus to a colander to drain, then pat dry with paper towels. Wrap well and refrigerate up to 24 hours.

Green, Yellow, or Snap Beans: Look for a bright color and firm texture without blemishes. Very fresh beans can be served uncooked. For blanching, trim ends of beans and cook in a large amount of boiling salted water for 1 to 2 minutes,

depending on the beans' size and freshness. Immediately rinse under cold running water. Pat dry. Wrap well and refrigerate up to 24 hours.

Broccoli: Broccoli should have tightly bunched, blue-green florets and firm stalks without signs of yellow buds or open cores at the base. For crudités, florets are best. Broccoli can be served raw or blanched. Cut the broccoli about 2½ inches down from the top of the florets, then divide the stems into small clusters with a small paring knife. For blanching, cook florets in a large amount of rapidly boiling salted water for 2 to 3 minutes. Gently drain in a large colander and cool under cold running water. Drain well and pat dry. Wrap well and refrigerate up to 24 hours.

Carrots: Available all year, carrots that still have their green leafy tops are worth seeking out. For fresh or packaged carrots, look for crisp, firm flesh and a

deep orange color. Baby carrots are also widely available and make a festive addition to your crudité platter. Carrots should be served raw, peeled, and cut into sticks or diagonally sliced. For extra crispness, place carrot sticks in enough ice water to cover and refrigerate several hours before serving.

Cauliflower: Look for creamy white, tightly packed florets without any signs of browning, and a bright green stalk. Raw or blanched cauliflower is wonderful for crudités. Remove the outer green leaves and core with a small paring knife, then divide florets into 1- to 1½-inch pieces. For blanching, cook florets in a large pot of salted boiling water for 2 to 3 minutes, depending on the size of florets. Gently drain in a large colander and cool under cold running water. Drain well and pat dry. Wrap well and refrigerate up to 24 hours.

Celery: Look for crisp, firm stalks with bright green leaves. Avoid celery with outer stalks that show signs of cracking or browning. Peel the tough outer stalks to remove the strings if desired, then cut into sticks and serve raw. For extra crispness, place celery sticks in enough ice water to cover and refrigerate several hours before serving.

Cherry Tomatoes: Red or yellow cherry tomatoes make a wonderful addition to a platter of crudités during the summer and early fall months. Look for bright colors, firm flesh, and green stems still attached. Unless the tomatoes are overripe, store at room temperature.

Cucumber: The majority of cucumbers are waxed, so you'll need to peel them. Select smaller, narrower cucumbers that are firm and dark green. Avoid cucumbers that have softened or are yellowed and pitted. Remove the seeds from larger cucumbers before cutting them into slices or sticks. We also recommend European or hot house cucumbers, which are becoming more widely available. This is a long, narrow variety of cucumber with a tender skin and does not need to be peeled or seeded.

Endive: Heads should be firm, crisp, and creamy white. Avoid heads with brown or limp outer leaves. Cut the head at the core then carefully separate the whole leaves for serving. Whole heads can be refrigerated, covered, up to 3 days.

Fennel (Anise): Look for firm, creamy colored bulbs with some of the stems and leaves attached. Trim the stems, then quarter the bulb and remove the core. Cut into thick slices and serve raw. For fennel, fresh is best so once you have sliced them, fennel sticks need to be served immediately.

Peppers: With a wide variety of colors to choose from—green, red, yellow, orange, and even purple—peppers are a colorful addition to a crudité platter. Look for firm peppers with shiny skin and deep color. Cut in half, remove seeds, and core and cut into strips or wedges. Once cut, peppers can be wrapped and refrigerated up to 24 hours.

Radishes: Ideally, look for radishes with attached greens. They should be brightly colored, and small or medium-sized. Serve whole with crudités, trimming the root and stem ends. Crisp in enough ice water to cover for 1 hour or overnight before serving.

BABA GHANOUSH

This classic dip from the Middle East can be garnished with pomegranate seeds, chopped fresh mint, or chopped pistachio nuts. It's always served with wedges of pita bread. Try our crisp Garlic Pita Chips (recipe, page 31).

▼ *Low-fat*
▽ *Low-calorie*
   Prep time: 15 minutes
   Baking time: 25 minutes
○ *Degree of difficulty: easy*

1 **large eggplant (about 1½ pounds)**
2 **tablespoons fresh lemon juice**
2 **tablespoons tahini (sesame paste)**
1 **tablespoon olive oil**
1 **teaspoon minced garlic**
1 **teaspoon salt**
2 **tablespoons chopped fresh parsley**
   Toasted pitas *or* Garlic Pita Chips
   (recipe, page 31)

1 Preheat oven to 400°F. Line a cookie sheet with foil. Halve the eggplant lengthwise and place cut side down on prepared sheet. Prick skin all over with a fork. Bake 25 minutes or until tender when pierced with a fork.

2 Remove eggplant peel with a small knife. Transfer pulp to a food processor and add the lemon juice, tahini, olive oil, garlic, and salt, then process until smooth. Transfer dip to a bowl and stir in the parsley. Serve with toasted pitas or Garlic Pita Chips. Makes 2 cups.

PER TABLESPOON		DAILY GOAL
Calories	14	2,000 (F), 2,500 (M)
Total fat	1 g	60 g or less (F), 70 g or less (M)
Saturated fat	0 g	20 g or less (F), 23 g or less (M)
Cholesterol	0 mg	300 mg or less
Sodium	70 mg	2,400 mg or less
Carbohydrates	1 g	250 g or more
Protein	0 g	55 g to 90 g

HUMMUS

Here's another classic dip from the Middle East that gets its creaminess from puréed chickpeas.

   Prep time: 10 minutes
○ *Degree of difficulty: easy*

1 **can (19 ounces) chickpeas (garbanzo beans), drained and rinsed**
⅓ **cup tahini (sesame paste)**
3 **tablespoons fresh lemon juice**
1½ **teaspoons minced garlic**
¼ **teaspoon freshly ground pepper**
   Pinch salt
¼ **cup olive oil**
   Toasted pita wedges *or* Garlic Pita Chips (recipe, page 31)

Combine the chickpeas, tahini, lemon juice, garlic, pepper, and salt in a food processor. With machine on, add the oil through feed tube in a steady stream and process about 30 seconds or until smooth. (Can be made ahead. Cover and refrigerate up to 24 hours.) Serve with toasted pita wedges or Garlic Pita Chips. Makes 2 cups.

PER TABLESPOON		DAILY GOAL
Calories	40	2,000 (F), 2,500 (M)
Total fat	3 g	60 g or less (F), 70 g or less (M)
Saturated fat	0 g	20 g or less (F), 23 g or less (M)
Cholesterol	0 mg	300 mg or less
Sodium	25 mg	2,400 mg or less
Carbohydrates	2 g	250 g or more
Protein	1 g	55 g to 90 g

SESAME-WHITE BEAN DIP

Tahini (sesame paste, available at many supermarkets and gourmet and health-foods shops) lends this dip a Middle Eastern flavor. A little goes a long way, so store any remaining tahini in the refrigerator once the container is opened.

Prep time: 10 minutes
Degree of difficulty: easy

1 **can (19 ounces) white kidney *or* cannellini beans, drained and rinsed**
¼ **cup tahini (sesame paste)**
2 **tablespoons fresh lemon juice**
¼ **teaspoon salt**
¼ **teaspoon freshly ground pepper**
¼ **cup olive oil**
¼ **cup chopped green onions**
1 **tablespoon sesame seeds, toasted**
  Garlic Pita Chips (recipe, page 31)
  Assorted fresh vegetables

Combine the beans, tahini, lemon juice, salt, and pepper in a food processor. With machine on, add the oil through feed tube in a steady stream and process about 30 seconds or until smooth. Stir in the green onions. (Can be made ahead. Cover and refrigerate up to 24 hours.) Sprinkle with sesame seeds. Serve with Garlic Pita Chips and assorted fresh vegetables. Makes 2 cups.

PER TABLESPOON		DAILY GOAL
Calories	40	2,000 (F), 2,500 (M)
Total fat	3 g	60 g or less (F), 70 g or less (M)
Saturated fat	0 g	20 g or less (F), 23 g or less (M)
Cholesterol	0 mg	300 mg or less
Sodium	40 mg	2,400 mg or less
Carbohydrates	3 g	250 g or more
Protein	1 g	55 g to 90 g

GUACAMOLE WITH A KICK

We've doubled the heat in this classic avocado dip with a jalapeño chile and hot pepper sauce.

▽ *Low-calorie*
   Prep time: 15 minutes plus chilling
○ *Degree of difficulty: easy*

1 **ripe avocado, peeled and pit removed**
½ **cup seeded and chopped tomato**
2 **tablespoons chopped green onion**
2 **tablespoons chopped fresh cilantro**
1 **tablespoon fresh lime juice**
2 **teaspoons seeded and minced jalapeño chile**
½ **teaspoon salt**
¼ **to ½ teaspoon hot pepper sauce**
   Tortilla chips *or* Oven-Baked Tortilla Chips (recipe, page 31)

Mash the avocado with a fork in a medium bowl. Stir in the tomato, green onion, cilantro, lime juice, jalapeño, salt, and hot pepper sauce. Serve immediately with tortilla chips or Oven-Baked Tortilla Chips. Makes 1⅓ cups.

PER TABLESPOON		DAILY GOAL
Calories	16	2,000 (F), 2,500 (M)
Total fat	1 g	60 g or less (F), 70 g or less (M)
Saturated fat	0 g	20 g or less (F), 23 g or less (M)
Cholesterol	0 mg	300 mg or less
Sodium	56 mg	2,400 mg or less
Carbohydrates	1 g	250 g or more
Protein	0 g	55 g to 90 g

NOTES

CHILE CON QUESO DIP

Punch the pause button on your VCR and whip up this dip! Thanks to the microwave, it's ready in minutes.

Ⓜ *Microwave*
Prep time: 15 minutes
Microwave time: 7 minutes
Ⓞ *Degree of difficulty: easy*

1 **tablespoon butter *or* margarine**
1 **can (4 ounces) chopped green chiles, drained**
½ **cup finely chopped onion**
1 **teaspoon minced garlic**
¼ **teaspoon freshly ground pepper Pinch cumin**
1 **cup canned tomatoes, chopped**
½ **pound Monterey Jack cheese, shredded (2 cups)**
1 **package (3 ounces) cream cheese, cubed**
1 **tablespoon chopped fresh cilantro Tortilla chips *or* Oven-Baked Tortilla Chips (recipe, page 31)**

1 Melt the butter in a medium microwave-proof bowl on high (100% power) 30 seconds. Add the chiles, onion, garlic, pepper, and cumin. Cover with plastic wrap, turning back a section to vent steam. Microwave on high (100% power) 2 minutes. Stir in the tomatoes and microwave, covered, on high (100% power) 2 minutes more.

2 Add the Monterey Jack and cream cheese. Cover and microwave on high (100% power) for 1 minute, then stir. Microwave 1 minute more, stirring until cheeses are melted. Stir in the cilantro. Serve with tortilla chips or Oven-Baked Tortilla Chips. Makes 2½ cups.

PER TABLESPOON		DAILY GOAL
Calories	35	2,000 (F), 2,500 (M)
Total fat	3 g	60 g or less (F), 70 g or less (M)
Saturated fat	2 g	20 g or less (F), 23 g or less (M)
Cholesterol	9 mg	300 mg or less
Sodium	67 mg	2,400 mg or less
Carbohydrates	1 g	250 g or more
Protein	2 g	55 g to 90 g

NOTES

28

CLASSIC SALSA CRUDA

Many bottled salsas are as low in calories and fat as this, but none delivers the same home-made, fresh from-the-garden flavor.

▼ *Low-fat*
▽ *Low-calorie*
  Prep time: 10 minutes
○ *Degree of difficulty: easy*

1 cup seeded and diced plum
    tomatoes
2 tablespoons chopped fresh cilantro
1 tablespoon minced red onion
1 tablespoon fresh lime juice
1 jalapeño chile, seeded and minced
⅛ to ¼ teaspoon salt
    Oven-Baked Tortilla Chips
      (recipe, page 31)

Stir together the tomato, cilantro, onion, lime juice, jalapeño, and salt in a small bowl. Serve with Oven-Baked Tortilla Chips. Makes about 1 cup.

PER ¼ CUP		DAILY GOAL
Calories	10	2,000 (F), 2,500 (M)
Total Fat	0 g	60 g or less (F), 70 g or less (M)
Saturated fat	0 g	20 g or less (F), 23 g or less (M)
Cholesterol	0 mg	300 mg or less
Sodium	106 mg	2,400 mg or less
Carbohydrates	3 g	250 g or more
Protein	1 g	55 g to 90 g

SALSA VERDE

This vibrant green dip features the tomatillo, a native fruit of Mexico. Found conveniently canned, tomatillos are now widely available in specialty food shops and Hispanic markets.

▼ *Low-fat*
▽ *Low-calorie*
  Prep time: 15 minutes
○ *Degree of difficulty: easy*

1   **can (18 ounces) tomatillos, drained**
1   **cup packed fresh cilantro**
2   **jalapeño chiles, minced**
1   **teaspoon granulated sugar
Tortilla chips *or* Oven-Baked Tortilla Chips (recipe, opposite page)**

Combine the tomatillos, cilantro, jalapeño, and sugar in a food processor or blender and process until chopped fine. Serve with tortilla chips or Oven-Baked Tortilla Chips. Makes 1⅓ cups.

PER TEASPOON		DAILY GOAL
Calories	2	2,000 (F), 2,500 (M)
Total fat	0 g	60 g or less (F), 70 g or less (M)
Saturated fat	0 g	20 g or less (F), 23 g or less (M)
Cholesterol	0 mg	300 mg or less
Sodium	17 mg	2,400 mg or less
Carbohydrates	0 g	250 g or more
Protein	0 g	55 g to 90 g

NOTES

GARLIC TOASTS

▼ *Low-fat*
Prep time: 15 minutes
Grilling time: 2 minutes
○ *Degree of difficulty: easy*

1 **loaf (1 pound) French *or* Italian bread, split lengthwise**
1 **garlic clove, peeled and halved**

Prepare grill or preheat broiler. Grill the bread 1 to 2 minutes, until deep golden. Rub the garlic clove over the cut sides of bread. Slice ½-inch thick. Makes 8 servings.

PER SERVING		DAILY GOAL
Calories	155	2,000 (F), 2,500 (M)
Total fat	2 g	60 g or less (F), 70 g or less (M)
Saturated fat	0 g	20 g or less (F), 23 g or less (M)
Cholesterol	0 mg	300 mg or less
Sodium	345 mg	2,400 mg or less
Carbohydrates	29 g	250 g or more
Protein	5 g	55 g to 90 g

GARLIC PITA CHIPS

These fragrant toasts are a perfect match with our Grilled Eggplant, Baba Ghanoush, Sesame-White Bean, and Hummus dips, or munch on them all on their own.

Prep time: 10 minutes
Baking time: 10 minutes
○ *Degree of difficulty: easy*

¼ **cup butter *or* margarine**
1½ **teaspoons minced garlic**
¼ **teaspoon freshly ground pepper**
4 **white *or* whole wheat pitas, split**

Preheat oven to 400°F. Melt the butter in a small saucepan over low heat with the garlic and pepper. Brush melted butter on cut side of pita halves. Cut each half into 6 wedges and place buttered side up on a cookie sheet. Bake 10 minutes or until toasted. (Can be made ahead. Wrap well and store at room temperature up to 2 days.) Makes 4 dozen.

PER CHIP		DAILY GOAL
Calories	25	2,000 (F), 2,500 (M)
Total fat	1 g	60 g or less (F), 70 g or less (M)
Saturated fat	.5 g	20 g or less (F), 23 g or less (M)
Cholesterol	3 mg	300 mg or less
Sodium	40 mg	2,400 mg or less
Carbohydrates	3 g	250 g or more
Protein	1 g	55 g to 90 g

OVEN-BAKED TORTILLA CHIPS

Prep time: 5 minutes
Cooking time: 5 to 7 minutes
○ *Degree of difficulty: easy*

8 **corn tortillas**

Preheat oven to 450°F. Cut each tortilla into 8 wedges and spread on 2 cookie sheets. Bake 5 to 7 minutes until crisp. Makes 4 servings.

PER SERVING		DAILY GOAL
Calories	110	2,000 (F), 2,500 (M)
Total fat	1 g	60 g or less (F), 70 g or less (M)
Saturated fat	0 g	20 g or less (F), 23 g or less (M)
Cholesterol	0 mg	300 mg or less
Sodium	80 mg	2,400 mg or less
Carbohydrates	23 g	250 g or more
Protein	3 g	55 g to 90 g

GLORIOUS

ANTIPASTO

Mangia! Come break the bread and celebrate the cuisines of the sun with this collection of warm and gutsy appetizers from the Mediterranean. Each, almost a meal in itself, can stand alone or be paired in a multitude of combinations for the perfect casual feast. This assortment features savory Tuscan Beans, Braised Artichokes with Mint, Baked Ricotta with Red Pepper Chutney, or Pissaladiére with tomatoes and anchovies.

CHEESE CROSTINI

These hors d'oeuvres are a tricolor salute to three regions of Italy: Naples, the home of mozzarella; southern Italy, where olives are especially revered; and Tuscany, where every cook makes a version of chicken liver crostini.

▼   *Low-fat*
▽   *Low-calorie*
   Prep time: 15 to 25 minutes plus standing
   Baking time: 8 to 11 minutes
○   *Degree of difficulty: easy*

½ **pound fresh mozzarella, diced**
1 **tablespoon extra-virgin olive oil**
1 **tablespoon chopped fresh basil**
¼ **teaspoon red pepper flakes**
2 **narrow loaves Italian *or* French bread, sliced into 12 slices each**

1 For mozzarella topping, combine the mozzarella, oil, basil, and red pepper in a medium bowl. Let stand at room temperature 1 hour.

2 Preheat oven to 400°F. Arrange the sliced bread on 2 cookie sheets and bake for 5 to 8 minutes or until lightly toasted, turning once. Spoon about 1 tablespoon mozzarella topping onto prepared toasts and bake about 3 minutes more or until cheese just begins to melt. Makes 24 appetizers.

PER APPETIZER		DAILY GOAL
Calories	110	2,000 (F), 2,500 (M)
Total fat	3 g	60 g or less (F), 70 g or less (M)
Saturated fat	0 g	20 g or less (F), 23 g or less (M)
Cholesterol	7 mg	300 mg or less
Sodium	173 mg	2,400 mg or less
Carbohydrates	16 g	250 g or more
Protein	4 g	55 g to 90 g

OLIVE PASTE CROSTINI

   Prep time: 15 minutes
   Baking time: 5 to 8 minutes
○   *Degree of difficulty: easy*

2 **narrow loaves Italian *or* French bread, sliced into 12 slices each**
4 **ounces Gaeta olives, pitted**
1 **tablespoon capers**
3 **anchovy fillets**
1 **tablespoon olive oil**
¼ **teaspoon minced garlic**

1 Preheat oven to 400°F. Arrange the sliced bread on 2 cookie sheets and bake for 5 to 8 minutes or until lightly toasted, turning once.

2 Place pitted olives, capers, anchovy fillets, olive oil, and garlic in a blender. Blend until smooth. Spread 1 teaspoon topping on each toast slice. Makes 24 appetizers.

PER APPETIZER		DAILY GOAL
Calories	90	2,000 (F), 2,500 (M)
Total fat	1 g	60 g or less (F), 70 g or less (M)
Saturated fat	0 g	20 g or less (F), 23 g or less (M)
Cholesterol	1 mg	300 mg or less
Sodium	35 mg	2,400 mg or less
Carbohydrates	16 g	250 g or more
Protein	3 g	55 g to 90 g

NOTES

_____

_____

_____

_____

_____

_____

_____

_____

CHICKEN LIVER CROSTINI

Prep time: 20 minutes
Baking time: 5 to 8 minutes
○ *Degree of difficulty: easy*

2   narrow loaves Italian *or* French bread, sliced into 12 slices each
1   tablespoon olive oil
½   pound chicken livers, trimmed
½   teaspoon sage
½   teaspoon salt
¼   teaspoon freshly ground pepper
1   tablespoon butter
¼   cup minced onion
2   tablespoons brandy
1   tablespoon chopped fresh parsley

1 Preheat oven to 400°F. Arrange the sliced bread on 2 cookie sheets and bake for 5 to 8 minutes or until lightly toasted, turning once.

2 Heat oil in a medium skillet over high heat. Add chicken livers. Sprinkle with sage, salt, and pepper. Cook, stirring, until livers are browned. Transfer to a medium bowl. Melt the butter in the skillet. Add onion and cook about 3 minutes or until tender. Return livers to skillet with brandy, then cook over high heat until brandy is evaporated. Remove from heat and mash with a spoon until blended. Spread 1 tablespoon liver mixture on each toast slice and sprinkle with parsley. Makes 24 appetizers.

PER APPETIZER		DAILY GOAL
Calories	115	2,000 (F), 2,500 (M)
Total fat	2 g	60 g or less (F), 70 g or less (M)
Saturated fat	1 g	20 g or less (F), 23 g or less (M)
Cholesterol	65 mg	300 mg or less
Sodium	254 mg	2,400 mg or less
Carbohydrates	17 g	250 g or more
Protein	5 g	55 g to 90 g

PISSALADIÉRE

This classic appetizer from the south of France is from none other than Julia Child. Her advice is to "be sure the onions are perfectly cooked and tender, since their sojourn in the oven is short." *Also pictured on page 32.*

Prep time: 35 minutes plus rising
Cooking time: 50 minutes
Degree of difficulty: moderate

Dough

- 1 package (¼ ounce) active dry yeast
- ½ cup warm water (105°F. to 115°F.)
- ⅛ teaspoon granulated sugar
- ¾ cup milk
- 2 tablespoons olive oil
- 1½ teaspoons salt
- 3 cups all-purpose flour

Topping

- 4 cups sliced onions
- ¼ cup plus 2 tablespoons olive oil, divided
- ¼ teaspoon thyme
  Salt
  Freshly ground pepper
- 2 large garlic cloves, minced
- 2 cans (2 ounces each) flat anchovy fillets, packed in oil, drained, divided
- ½ cup freshly grated Parmesan cheese, divided
- ½ cup Niçoise olives
  Fresh thyme sprigs, for garnish

1 For dough, stir the yeast, warm water, and sugar in a large bowl and let stand 5 minutes or until foamy. Blend the milk, oil, and salt into the yeast mixture.

2 Gradually stir the flour into the yeast mixture. Turn onto a lightly floured surface and knead for 8 to 10 minutes or until smooth and elastic.

3 Cover and let rest in a warm, draft-free place until doubled in bulk, about 1½ hours. Shape and bake immediately or punch down dough and refrigerate up to 1 hour.

4 Meanwhile, for the topping, cook the onions in the ¼ cup olive oil in a large skillet about 30 minutes or until very tender. Remove from heat and season with the thyme, and salt and pepper to taste. Cool. Mash the garlic with 6 of the anchovies and the remaining 2 tablespoons of oil. Set aside. Cut the remaining anchovies into thin strips.

5 Preheat oven to 450°F. Place a heavy cookie sheet on the middle oven rack. When warm, remove sheet from oven and brush with oil. Roll dough into a 12-inch square on a lightly floured surface. Place on warm cookie sheet. Spread anchovy mixture evenly over dough. Layer with ¼ cup of the Parmesan, the onions, olives, then the remaining ¼ cup Parmesan. Top with anchovy strips and thyme sprigs. Bake about 15 minutes or until crust is golden. Cut into 2-inch squares. Makes 3 dozen appetizers.

PER SQUARE		DAILY GOAL
Calories	90	2,000 (F), 2,500 (M)
Total fat	4 g	60 g or less (F), 70 g or less (M)
Saturated fat	1 g	20 g or less (F), 23 g or less (M)
Cholesterol	3 mg	300 mg or less
Sodium	228 mg	2,400 mg or less
Carbohydrates	10 g	250 g or more
Protein	3 g	55 g to 90 g

FOCACCIA

One of the hottest breads around is also one of the oldest! Focaccia (derived from "focus," the Latin word for hearth) was originally baked in fireplace ashes. It's great for eating plain or with sliced mozzarella and tomatoes.

Prep time: 35 minutes plus rising
Baking time: 20 to 30 minutes
Degree of difficulty: moderate

- 1 **package active dry yeast**
- 2 **cups warm water (105°F. to 115°F.), divided**
- 5 **to 5½ cups bread or all-purpose flour, divided**
- 1½ **teaspoons salt**
- 6 **tablespoons extra-virgin olive oil, divided**
- 1 **teaspoon kosher or sea salt**
- 2 **teaspoons assorted chopped fresh herbs such as sage, rosemary, and thyme, or 1 teaspoon assorted dried herbs**

1 Sprinkle the yeast over 1 cup of the warm water in a large mixing bowl. Stir briefly, then let stand 5 minutes to dissolve. Attach paddle or dough hook to mixer. At low speed, stir in 2 cups of the flour and the salt. Beat about 1 minute more or until smooth. (Or, combine ingredients in a large bowl and beat vigorously with a wooden spoon for 2 minutes.) Add the remaining 1 cup of water and 3 tablespoons of the oil to blend. Add enough flour, ½ cup at a time, to make a soft dough that begins to pull away from the sides of the bowl.

2 On a lightly floured surface, knead dough for 8 to 10 minutes or until smooth and elastic. Place dough in a large, lightly greased bowl, turning to grease top. Cover with a kitchen towel and let rise in a warm, draft-free place for 1 to 1¼ hours or until doubled in bulk. Remove dough from bowl and gently knead 1 minute.

3 Lightly oil a 15x10½-inch jelly-roll pan. With a lightly floured rolling pin, roll dough into a 12x8-inch rectangle. Carefully transfer to prepared pan, stretching it gently to edges of pan with fingers. Press top of dough with fingertips, leaving ½-inch-deep indentations. Cover and let rise 30 minutes.

4 Preheat oven to 425°F. Adjust 1 oven rack to lowest position. Place a shallow baking pan on the top rack of the oven. (If using a baking stone,* place in cold oven and preheat for 30 minutes before baking.) Press dough again with fingers and brush with 1 tablespoon of the olive oil. Sprinkle with the salt and herbs.

5 Just before baking, carefully place 1 cup ice cubes in baking pan on the top oven rack and immediately place the dough on the baking stone on lowest oven rack. Bake for 20 to 25 minutes, if using stone (25 to 30 minutes if not) or until top is golden and bottom sounds hollow when removed from pan and tapped on bottom. Remove Focaccia from pan and transfer to a wire rack. While still warm, brush top with the remaining 2 tablespoons olive oil. Cool. Cut into 5x1½-inch pieces. Makes 35 appetizers.

*Baking stones can be ordered from The King Arthur Flour Baker's Catalogue, PO Box 876, Norwich, VT 05055-0876; or call 1-800-827-6836.

PER APPETIZER		DAILY GOAL
Calories	95	2,000 (F), 2,500 (M)
Total fat	3 g	60 g or less (F), 70 g or less (M)
Saturated fat	1 g	20 g or less (F), 23 g or less (M)
Cholesterol	0 mg	300 mg or less
Sodium	137 mg	2,400 mg or less
Carbohydrates	14 g	250 g or more
Protein	2 g	55 g to 90 g

ROASTED RED PEPPER BAGUETTE

This spicy hors d'oeuvre with tangy goat cheese, balsamic vinegar, and roasted red peppers is finished in a jiffy and great for last-minute entertaining.

Prep time: 10 minutes
Broiling time: 5 minutes
Degree of difficulty: easy

- 1 loaf (1 pound) French bread
- 2 jars (7 ounces each) roasted red peppers, drained and sliced
- ⅓ cup pitted ripe olives
- ¼ cup extra-virgin olive oil
- ¼ cup minced shallots
- 2 tablespoons balsamic vinegar
- 1 tablespoon chopped fresh parsley
- ½ teaspoon freshly ground pepper
- ¼ teaspoon salt
- 4 ounces goat cheese, crumbled

1 Preheat broiler. Slice the bread in half lengthwise and place cut side up on a broiler pan.

2 Combine the red peppers, olives, oil, shallots, vinegar, parsley, pepper, and salt in a medium bowl, stirring to mix well. Spoon evenly over cut sides of bread halves, then top with the goat cheese. Broil 3 inches from heat source about 5 minutes or until cheese begins to soften and edges of bread are lightly browned. Cut into 1-inch slices and serve. Makes 40 appetizers.

PER APPETIZER		DAILY GOAL
Calories	60	2,000 (F), 2,500 (M)
Total fat	3 g	60 g or less (F), 70 g or less (M)
Saturated fat	1 g	20 g or less (F), 23 g or less (M)
Cholesterol	2 mg	300 mg or less
Sodium	108 mg	2,400 mg or less
Carbohydrates	7 g	250 g or more
Protein	2 g	55 g to 90 g

BAKED RICOTTA

Baked ricotta imported from Italy is quite a delicacy and not always available so we decided to make it ourselves. It couldn't be easier. Just shape it and bake it and serve with our savory Red Pepper Chutney (recipe, page 42), assorted breads, and crudités.

Prep time: 5 minutes plus chilling
Baking time: 1 hour
○ *Degree of difficulty: easy*

1 **large container (45 ounces) whole milk ricotta cheese**

1 Line a large sieve with a double layer of cheesecloth, letting the excess overhang sides, and place over a bowl. Spoon in the ricotta. Cover and allow to drain in the refrigerator overnight.

2 Preheat oven to 400°F. Discard drained liquid in the bowl. Using cheesecloth, lift ricotta and transfer to a 1½-quart oven-proof bowl, Charlotte mold, or soufflé dish, letting cheesecloth overhang. Bake 1 hour or until top is browned. Cool on a wire rack 15 minutes. Lift ricotta and cheesecloth from bowl and drain again in sieve 30 minutes. Wrap and refrigerate at least 3 hours. (Can be made ahead. Cover and refrigerate up to 48 hours.) Just before serving, peel off cheesecloth. Makes 24 servings.

PER SERVING		DAILY GOAL
Calories	100	2,000 (F), 2,500 (M)
Total fat	7 g	60 g or less (F), 70 g or less (M)
Saturated fat	5 g	20 g or less (F), 23 g or less (M)
Cholesterol	29 mg	300 mg or less
Sodium	48 mg	2,400 mg or less
Carbohydrates	2 g	250 g or more
Protein	6 g	55 g to 90 g

NOTES

RED PEPPER CHUTNEY

The key to the sweet flavor of this spread is cooking the onions very slowly over low heat.

Prep time: 15 minutes
Cooking time: 1 hour 10 minutes
○ *Degree of difficulty: easy*

2 tablespoons olive oil
4 cups finely chopped sweet white onions (about 2 pounds)

3 large red peppers, finely chopped (4 cups)
1 teaspoon salt
½ teaspoon red pepper flakes
¼ teaspoon fennel seeds
½ cup cider vinegar
¼ cup granulated sugar
2 tablespoons chopped fresh parsley
Assorted breads and crudités

1 Heat the oil in a large skillet over medium-low heat. Add the onions; cover and cook, stirring occasionally, about 45 minutes or until very tender and just beginning to brown. Stir in the red peppers, salt, pepper flakes, and fennel seeds and cook, covered, stirring occasionally, 15 minutes.

2 Increase heat to high. Add the vinegar and sugar and cook, stirring, about 10 minutes more or until almost dry. Cool. (Can be made ahead. Cover and refrigerate up to 3 days.) Stir in the parsley and serve with breads and crudités. Makes 3 cups.

PER TABLESPOON		DAILY GOAL
Calories	20	2,000 (F), 2,500 (M)
Total fat	1 g	60 g or less (F), 70 g or less (M)
Saturated fat	0 g	20 g or less (F), 23 g or less (M)
Cholesterol	0 mg	300 mg or less
Sodium	48 mg	2,400 mg or less
Carbohydrates	3 g	250 g or more
Protein	0 g	55 g to 90 g

THE ANTIPASTO PANTRY

Anchovies: In the U.S., anchovies are most available cured or packed in oil in jars or cans. Look for plump, firm fillets in the jar without murky oil.

Balsamic vinegar: This sweet vinegar has been made in Modena, Italy, for more than a thousand years. The best balsamic vinegar is rarely found outside Italy. Made purely from the cooked-down juices of white grapes, it is aged for decades in barrels of different woods. Balsamic vinegar that is exported is a blend of wine vinegar, reduced grape juice, and possibly some young balsamic vinegar and caramel coloring.

Olive oil: All olive oils are graded according to their level of acidity; the least acidic is extra-virgin. Extra-virgin and virgin olive oils are made from the first pressing of the olives. Both are used

TOMATO BRUSCHETTA

Grilled in summer or broiled in winter, this Italian bread can be served with an infinite variety of toppings. Here's a classic with tomatoes and basil.

Prep time: 10 minutes
Grilling time: 2 to 4 minutes
Degree of difficulty: easy

6   plum tomatoes, diced
2   tablespoons extra-virgin olive oil
2   tablespoons chopped fresh basil
¼   teaspoon salt

¼   teaspoon freshly ground pepper
6   large slices crusty Italian bread
2   garlic cloves, peeled and halved

Prepare grill or preheat broiler. Combine the tomatoes, oil, basil, salt, and pepper in a small bowl. Grill or broil bread until golden on both sides. Immediately rub 1 side of bread with cut garlic, then top slices evenly with tomato mixture. Makes 6 servings.

PER SERVING		DAILY GOAL
Calories	165	2,000 (F), 2,500 (M)
Total fat	6 g	60 g or less (F), 70 g or less (M)
Saturated fat	1 g	20 g or less (F), 23 g or less (M)
Cholesterol	0 mg	300 mg or less
Sodium	342 mg	2,400 mg or less
Carbohydrates	24 g	250 g or more
Protein	4 g	55 g to 90 g

in cooking, but the more expensive oils are best drizzled over grilled vegetables and in salad dressing. Olive oil (formerly called pure) is a blend of refined and virgin oil. Light olive oil, another blend, is light in color and flavor, not calories or fat.

Olives: You can choose from many varieties of olives to use in cooking. Gaeta olives are small, reddish brown, and similar to Niçoise olives. Oil-cured olives such as Kalamata, which are black with smooth skin, and large green olives from southern Italy are also good choices.

BAGNA CAUDA

Bagna Cauda (the translation is "warm bath") is delicious with any vegetable you choose—fresh fennel is a favorite of ours.

Prep time: 40 minutes
○ *Degree of difficulty: easy*

2 **large heads fennel, halved, cored, and cut lengthwise into 1-inch strips**
3 **peppers (1 red, 1 green, 1 yellow), cored, seeded, and cut into strips**
3 **heads Belgian endive, separated into leaves**
1 **pound baby carrots**
⅓ **cup extra-virgin olive oil**
½ **teaspoon minced garlic**
6 **tablespoons butter, cut up (no substitutions)**
1 **can (2 ounces) flat anchovy fillets, packed in oil, drained and chopped**

1 Arrange the vegetables on a large serving platter. Cover and refrigerate up to 8 hours.

2 For dip, heat the oil and garlic in a small saucepan over low heat just until garlic turns golden. Add the butter and anchovies and cook until butter melts. Serve hot with vegetables. Makes 12 servings.

PER SERVING WITH 1 TABLESPOON DIP		DAILY GOAL
Calories	145	2,000 (F), 2,500 (M)
Total fat	12 g	60 g or less (F), 70 g or less (M)
Saturated fat	4 g	20 g or less (F), 23 g or less (M)
Cholesterol	18 mg	300 mg or less
Sodium	279 mg	2,400 mg or less
Carbohydrates	7 g	250 g or more
Protein	3 g	55 g to 90 g

NOTES

GRILLED YELLOW PEPPERS WITH SALSA VERDE

Here's a glorious appetizer from Alice Waters, owner of Chez Panisse restaurant in Berkeley, California. Charring the skins of colored peppers gives them a sweet, smoky flavor. Chef Waters tops the peppers with Salsa Verde, a parsley-shallot sauce, and serves them with plenty of crunchy garlic bread.

Prep time: 40 minutes
Grilling time: 22 minutes
○ *Degree of difficulty: easy*

4 **large yellow peppers**
4 **large slices sourdough peasant bread, ½-inch thick**
4 **teaspoons olive oil**
1 **large clove garlic, peeled**

Salsa Verde
5 **tablespoons extra-virgin olive oil**
4 **anchovy fillets, rinsed, patted dry, and finely chopped**
2 **tablespoons chopped fresh parsley**
2 **tablespoons minced shallots**
1 **tablespoon capers, finely chopped**
1 **teaspoon chopped fresh tarragon**
1 **teaspoon chopped fresh oregano**
1 **teaspoon chopped fresh thyme**
¼ **teaspoon minced garlic**
1 **teaspoon white wine vinegar**
   Pinch salt
⅛ **teaspoon freshly ground pepper**

1 Prepare grill or preheat broiler. Grill the peppers over medium coals or broil 5 inches from heat source, turning occasionally, about 20 minutes or until completely charred but still firm. Transfer to a paper bag and let stand about 10 minutes or until cool enough to handle.

2 Meanwhile, brush the bread lightly on both sides with the oil and grill or broil about 30 seconds per side or until golden. Rub bread with the garlic clove.

3 For Salsa Verde, combine the oil, anchovies, parsley, shallots, capers, tarragon, oregano, thyme, and garlic in a small bowl. Stir in the vinegar, salt, and pepper.

4 When peppers are cooled, remove skin and seeds. Cut into 1-inch strips. Spoon Salsa Verde over peppers and serve with grilled bread. Makes 4 servings.

PER SERVING WITH 2 TABLESPOONS SALSA		DAILY GOAL
Calories	315	2,000 (F), 2,500 (M)
Total fat	24 g	60 g or less (F), 70 g or less (M)
Saturated fat	3 g	20 g or less (F), 23 g or less (M)
Cholesterol	2 mg	300 mg or less
Sodium	421 mg	2,400 mg or less
Carbohydrates	16 g	250 g or more
Protein	5 g	55 g to 90 g

NOTES

_____

_____

_____

_____

_____

_____

_____

_____

_____

BRAISED ARTICHOKES WITH MINT

Serve this Roman dish at room temperature as an irresistible antipasto.

Prep time: 20 minutes
Cooking time: 25 to 30 minutes
Degree of difficulty: moderate

3 **large** *or* 4 **small artichokes, quartered**
½ **cup water**
3 **tablespoons olive oil**
2 **tablespoons chopped fresh parsley**
1 **teaspoon minced garlic**
½ **teaspoon salt**
¼ **teaspoon dried mint**
¼ **cup chopped fresh mint**
1 **teaspoon minced lemon peel**

1 Remove outer leaves of the artichokes and trim stems to 1 inch, then peel stems with a small, sharp knife. Slice off top half of artichokes and cut out the fuzzy "choke" centers.

2 Arrange artichokes in a single layer in a medium skillet. Drizzle with the water and oil. Combine the parsley, garlic, salt, and dried mint in a cup and sprinkle evenly over artichokes; bring to a boil. Reduce heat and simmer, covered, for 20 to 25 minutes or until tender. Uncover and continue to cook until all but 2 tablespoons of liquid is evaporated.

3 Transfer artichokes and liquid to a serving dish. Combine the fresh mint and lemon peel in a cup and sprinkle on top. Makes 4 servings.

PER SERVING		DAILY GOAL	
Calories	150	2,000 (F), 2,500 (M)	
Total fat	10 g	60 g or less (F), 70 g or less (M)	
Saturated fat	1 g	20 g or less (F), 23 g or less (M)	
Cholesterol	0 mg	300 mg or less	
Sodium	389 mg	2,400 mg or less	
Carbohydrates	13 g	250 g or more	
Protein	4 g	55 g to 90 g	

INSALATA DI FRUTTI DI MARE

This salad features shrimp, scallops, squid, and mussels, but in Italy the kinds of fish may vary from region to region. Clams, crab, monkfish, and oysters all work well too.

Prep time: 35 minutes plus chilling
Cooking time: 25 minutes
O *Degree of difficulty: easy*

Dressing
- ¼ cup fresh lemon juice
- ¼ teaspoon minced garlic
- ½ teaspoon salt
- ⅛ teaspoon freshly ground pepper
- ¼ cup olive oil

Salad
- 2 cups water
- 1 carrot, cut up
- Half of 1 celery rib, cut into 2-inch pieces
- 1 garlic clove, crushed
- 6 peppercorns
- ½ small lemon, sliced
- ½ pound medium shrimp, peeled and deveined
- ½ pound sea scallops, halved
- ½ pound cleaned squid, sliced thin
- 1 pound small mussels, scrubbed
- 2 tablespoons chopped fresh parsley
  Lemon wedges, for garnish (optional)

1 For dressing, combine the lemon juice, garlic, salt, and pepper in a medium bowl. Slowly whisk in the oil until blended and set aside.

2 For salad, combine the water, carrot, celery, garlic, peppercorns, and lemon in a medium saucepan. Bring to a boil over high heat. Reduce heat to medium, then add the shrimp, cover and cook 2 minutes. With a slotted spoon, transfer shrimp to a large bowl. Return liquid to a boil, then add the scallops and cook for 2 minutes. Transfer to the bowl with the shrimp. Repeat with the squid, cooking 30 seconds. Return liquid to a boil, then add the mussels and cook, covered, over high heat for 5 minutes. Transfer opened mussels to a plate. Cover and cook remaining mussels 1 minute more. Discard any unopened mussels.

3 Remove mussels from shells and add to bowl with the other seafood. Add the dressing, tossing to coat. Cover and refrigerate at least 1 hour. (Can be made ahead. Cover and refrigerate up to 8 hours. Remove from refrigerator 30 minutes before serving.)

4 To serve, stir in the parsley. Garnish with lemon, if desired. Makes 6 servings.

PER SERVING		DAILY GOAL
Calories	210	2,000 (F), 2,500 (M)
Total fat	11 g	60 g or less (F), 70 g or less (M)
Saturated fat	2 g	20 g or less (F), 23 g or less (M)
Cholesterol	154 mg	300 mg or less
Sodium	376 mg	2,400 mg or less
Carbohydrates	6 g	250 g or more
Protein	21 g	55 g to 90 g

NOTES

_____

_____

_____

_____

_____

_____

QUICK RATATOUILLE SALAD

Peak season summer veggies are best in this salad, which is great served with Garlic Toasts (recipe, page 31).

▽ *Low-calorie*
   Prep time: 20 minutes
   Cooking time: 13 minutes
○ *Degree of difficulty: easy*

3 **cups diced tomatoes**
¼ **cup julienned fresh basil leaves**
½ **teaspoon salt**
¼ **teaspoon freshly ground pepper**
2 **tablespoons extra-virgin olive oil**
6 **cups diced eggplant**
4 **cups diced zucchini**
1 **teaspoon minced garlic**
   Julienned fresh basil, for garnish
      (optional)

1 Combine the tomatoes, basil, salt, and pepper in a large bowl.

2 Heat the oil in a large nonstick skillet over medium-high heat. Add the eggplant and cook, stirring occasionally, 8 minutes. Add the zucchini and garlic and cook about 5 minutes more or until vegetables are tender. Combine the cooked vegetables with tomato mixture and garnish with julienned basil, if desired. Makes 6 cups.

PER CUP		DAILY GOAL
Calories	95	2,000 (F), 2,500 (M)
Total fat	5 g	60 g or less (F), 70 g or less (M)
Saturated fat	1 g	20 g or less (F), 23 g or less (M)
Cholesterol	0 mg	300 mg or less
Sodium	197 mg	2,400 mg or less
Carbohydrates	12 g	250 g or more
Protein	3 g	55 g to 90 g

NOTES

CAPONATA

A classic eggplant relish from Sicily, Caponata is a combination of sweet and sour flavors lent by balsamic vinegar and capers. We also like to serve it with pita triangles and crackers.

▽ *Low-calorie*
Prep time: 20 minutes
Cooking time: 35 minutes
○ *Degree of difficulty: easy*

3 **tablespoons olive oil, divided**
1 **cup chopped onions**
2 **large cloves garlic, minced**
8 **ounces fresh mushrooms, chopped**
3 **cups diced eggplant**
3 **tablespoons balsamic vinegar**
1 **can (14 *or* 16 ounces) whole**
   tomatoes in juice
2 **tablespoons capers, drained**
2 **teaspoons granulated sugar**
½ **teaspoon salt**
¼ **teaspoon thyme**
⅛ **teaspoon red pepper flakes**
   Toasted semolina bread

1 Heat 1 tablespoon of the oil in a large skillet over medium heat. Add the onions and garlic and cook 4 to 5 minutes until softened.

2 Add another tablespoon of oil and the mushrooms to the pan and increase the heat to medium-high. Cook vegetables, stirring occasionally, 6 to 8 minutes or until mushrooms are tender. Add the remaining 1 tablespoon oil and the eggplant to the skillet, then cover and cook for 6 minutes more.

3 Add the vinegar and continue to cook uncovered, stirring, until evaporated. Add the tomatoes and their liquid, breaking up the tomatoes with a spoon. Stir in the capers, sugar, salt, thyme, and pepper flakes. Simmer for 15 to 20 minutes or until eggplant is completely tender and mixture is thick.

4 Transfer mixture to a food processor. Process, pulsing on and off 3 to 4 times, just until coarsely chopped. Transfer to a serving bowl. Spread on semolina bread. Makes 3 cups.

PER TABLESPOON		DAILY GOAL
Calories	15	2,000 (F), 2,500 (M)
Total fat	1 g	60 g or less (F), 70 g or less (M)
Saturated fat	0 g	20 g or less (F), 23 g or less (M)
Cholesterol	0 mg	300 mg or less
Sodium	47 mg	2,400 mg or less
Carbohydrates	1 g	250 g or more
Protein	0 g	55 g to 90 g

NOTES

HERBED OLIVES

There's an elegant simplicity to these herbed olives, and the recipe, from cookbook author and food writer Nancy Verde Barr, of Providence, Rhode Island, couldn't be easier. Baking the olives deepens their flavor and the choice of herbs is up to you. The oil that the olives are stored in is also perfect for salad dressings.

Prep time: 5 minutes
Baking time: 30 minutes
○ *Degree of difficulty: easy*

1 **pound brine-cured black olives (such as Gaeta *or* Kalamata), drained**

3 **large garlic cloves, peeled and smashed**

3 **sprigs (3 inches each) fresh rosemary *or* 1 teaspoon fennel seeds**

1 **sprig (2 inches) fresh thyme**

1 **small dried red chile *or* ½ teaspoon red pepper flakes**
 Extra-virgin olive oil

1 Preheat oven to 325°F. Spread the olives, garlic, rosemary, thyme, and chile in a shallow 2-quart casserole or 9-inch square baking dish. Pour ¾ cup oil on top. Bake 30 minutes, stirring occasionally. Cool to room temperature.

2 Spoon the olive mixture into 3 sterilized, ½-pint jars and add additional oil to cover completely. Cover and store in the refrigerator up to 1 month. Makes 3 cups.

PER OUNCE (10 MEDIUM OLIVES)		DAILY GOAL
Calories	65	2,000 (F), 2,500 (M)
Total fat	7 g	60 g or less (F), 70 g or less (M)
Saturated fat	1 g	20 g or less (F), 23 g or less (M)
Cholesterol	0 mg	300 mg or less
Sodium	248 mg	2,400 mg or less
Carbohydrates	2 g	250 g or more
Protein	0 g	55 g to 90 g

NOTES

TUSCAN BEANS

This rustic dish is made with cannellini, or white kidney beans, the most popular beans in Italian cooking. It makes a great topping for Garlic Toasts (recipe, page 31).

▼ *Low-fat*
Prep time: 5 minutes plus standing
Cooking time: 50 to 60 minutes
○ *Degree of difficulty: easy*

1½ **cups dried cannellini *or* Great Northern beans, rinsed**
1 **can (13¾ *or* 14½ ounces) chicken broth**
1½ **cups water**
½ **cup fresh sage leaves *or* 1 tablespoon dried sage plus 2 tablespoons chopped fresh parsley**
¼ **teaspoon freshly ground pepper**
1½ **teaspoons minced garlic**
2 **tablespoons olive oil**
¾ **teaspoon salt**

1 Soak the beans in water to cover by 2 inches in a large saucepan overnight. (Or, to quick-soak: Combine beans with water to cover by 2 inches in a large saucepan and bring to a boil; boil 2 minutes. Cover and let stand 1 hour.) Drain.

2 Combine the drained beans, broth, water, sage, and pepper in the saucepan; bring to a boil. Reduce heat, cover, and simmer about 40 minutes or until tender. Add the garlic, oil, and salt and simmer, uncovered, for 5 to 15 minutes more or until beans are tender but not mushy. Makes 4½ cups.

PER ½ CUP		DAILY GOAL
Calories	140	2,000 (F), 2,500 (M)
Total fat	4 g	60 g or less (F), 70 g or less (M)
Saturated fat	1 g	20 g or less (F), 23 g or less (M)
Cholesterol	0 mg	300 mg or less
Sodium	415 mg	2,400 mg or less
Carbohydrates	20 g	250 g or more
Protein	7 g	55 g to 90 g

SAY IT WITH CHEESE

Whatever cheese you choose for your antipasto—mozzarella, Parmesan, or fontina—what's most important is that it's served at the proper temperature. Quite often cheese is served too cold. If cheese is part of your antipasto buffet, we suggest you arrange it on a serving platter, cover it, and let it stand at room temperature for 1 hour before party time.

NOTES

_____

_____

_____

_____

_____

_____

_____

_____

_____

WHOLE ROASTED GARLIC

Don't be overwhelmed by the amount of garlic—slow cooking sweetens and mellows it.

Prep time: 5 minutes
Baking time: 1 to 1¼ hours
Degree of difficulty: easy

4 **whole medium heads garlic**
¼ **cup olive oil**
   Crusty bread *or* assorted fresh vegetables

1 Preheat oven to 350°F. Remove the outer skin from the garlic, keeping heads intact, and arrange right side up in an 8-inch square baking pan. Drizzle the oil over tops of garlic, letting it run between the cloves. Cover and bake 1 hour, basting occasionally, or until cloves are very soft and center is tender when tested with a toothpick. Cool

2 To serve, pull off cloves and gently squeeze garlic paste onto bread or vegetables. Makes 4 servings.

PER SERVING		DAILY GOAL
Calories	225	2,000 (F), 2,500 (M)
Total fat	14 g	60 g or less (F), 70 g or less (M)
Saturated fat	2 g	20 g or less (F), 23 g or less (M)
Cholesterol	0 mg	300 mg or less
Sodium	12 mg	2,400 mg or less
Carbohydrates	24 g	250 g or more
Protein	5 g	55 g to 90 g

BITES FROM

THE BAR

Do you have a favorite munchy served at your local watering hole? Or, is there a special appetizer you crave from a restaurant? If that's the case, you may just find the recipe here. There's everything from Fried Calamari with Creamy Salsa to melt-in-your-mouth Fried Mozzarella with Anchovy Dip. If you're looking for something on the spicy side, pull up a stool, grab an icy brew, and dig into four-alarm Pepper Jack Empanadas or Buffalo Chicken Wings.

BLACK BEAN SALSA

Almost a salad, this hearty salsa is a natural just rolled up in a soft flour tortilla.

▼ *Low-fat*
▽ *Low-calorie*
  Prep time: 25 minutes
  Cooking time: 1 to 1¼ hours
○ *Degree of difficulty: easy*

1 **cup dried black beans, picked over and rinsed**
  Half of 1 bay leaf
1 **garlic clove plus ½ teaspoon minced garlic, divided**
2 **teaspoons cumin**
¼ **teaspoon red pepper flakes**
2¼ **teaspoons salt, divided**
⅓ **cup finely diced onion**
1 **large tomato, seeded and diced**
⅓ **cup finely diced radishes**
2 **tablespoons chopped fresh cilantro**
1 **tablespoon fresh lime juice**
1 **teaspoon minced jalapeño *or* serrano chile**

1 In a large bowl, cover beans with 2 inches of water and soak overnight. (Or, to quick-soak: Combine beans and enough water to cover by 2 inches in a large saucepan and bring to a boil; boil 2 minutes. Cover and let stand 1 hour.) Drain, then cover with fresh water and bring to a boil. Add the bay leaf, the whole garlic clove, cumin, and pepper flakes. Reduce heat and simmer for 1 to 1¼ hours or until beans are tender. Remove beans from heat and stir in 2 teaspoons of the salt. Cool the beans in liquid. Drain beans, discarding the liquid, garlic, and bay leaf.

2 Rinse the onion in a fine sieve under cold water, then drain and pat dry on paper towels. Combine onion with drained cooked beans, the ½ teaspoon minced garlic, the remaining ¼ teaspoon salt, tomato, radishes, cilantro, lime juice, and chile. Makes 4 cups.

PER ¼ CUP		DAILY GOAL
Calories	45	2,000 (F), 2,500 (M)
Total fat	0 g	60 g or less (F), 70 g or less (M)
Saturated fat	0 g	20 g or less (F), 23 g or less (M)
Cholesterol	0 mg	300 mg or less
Sodium	174 mg	2,400 mg or less
Carbohydrates	9 g	250 g or more
Protein	3 g	55 g to 90 g

NOTES

GRILLED CORN AND CHILE SALSA

Charring the poblano chiles—large, medium-hot chile peppers—on the grill adds a rich, smoky flavor to this summer harvest salsa. The corn and zucchini cool things off.

▼ *Low-fat*
▽ *Low-calorie*
  Prep time: 35 minutes plus soaking
  Grilling time: 15 minutes
○ *Degree of difficulty: easy*

3 **ears corn**
2 **fresh poblano chiles**
1 **cup diced zucchini**
1 **plum tomato, seeded and finely diced**
¼ **cup thinly sliced green onions**
1 **tablespoon chopped fresh oregano** *or* ½ **teaspoon dried**
1 **tablespoon fresh lime juice**
1 **tablespoon olive oil**
½ **teaspoon minced garlic**
¼ **teaspoon salt**

1 Peel the husks of the corn down to the bottom of each ear without detaching and remove silk. Replace husks and secure with twine. Soak corn in a large bowl of cold water at least 30 minutes before grilling.

2 Prepare grill. Drain corn and grill corn and chiles, about 10 minutes for chiles and 15 minutes for corn, turning every 5 minutes, or until tender and evenly charred. Cover vegetables and let stand 10 minutes.

3 When cool enough to handle, peel the skin from the chiles, then discard membranes and seeds and cut chiles into fine dice. Remove husks from corn and discard. Carefully cut kernels from each cob, then transfer the corn to a medium bowl. Add diced chiles, zucchini, tomato, green onions, oregano, lime juice, oil, garlic, and salt. Makes 3½ cups.

PER ¼ CUP		DAILY GOAL
Calories	30	2,000 (F), 2,500 (M)
Total fat	1 g	60 g or less (F), 70 g or less (M)
Saturated fat	0 g	20 g or less (F), 23 g or less (M)
Cholesterol	0 mg	300 mg or less
Sodium	43 mg	2,400 mg or less
Carbohydrates	5 g	250 g or more
Protein	1 g	55 g to 90 g

NOTES

59

SOUTHWEST TACO DIP

The gang's going to love this one! Choose from a ground beef or turkey filling. We've replaced the traditional refried beans with spicy black beans.

Ⓜ *Microwave*
Prep time: 15 minutes
Microwave time: 10 minutes
Ⓞ *Degree of difficulty: easy*

2 **cans (15 ounces each) black beans, drained and rinsed**
¾ **pound lean ground beef *or* turkey**
½ **cup chopped onion**
1 **teaspoon chili powder**
1 **cup prepared salsa**
1 **cup shredded sharp cheddar cheese**
1 **container (8 ounces) sour cream**
3 **tablespoons chopped fresh cilantro**
¼ **teaspoon salt**
¼ **teaspoon freshly ground pepper**
1 **ripe avocado, peeled, pit removed, and finely chopped**
2 **plum tomatoes, finely chopped**
2 **green onions, sliced**
  Tortilla chips

1 Combine the beans, ground beef or turkey, onion, and chili powder in a shallow 2 quart microwave-proof dish. Cover with wax paper and microwave on high (100% power) about 8 minutes or until meat is cooked through, stirring to mash beans and break up meat every 3 minutes. Drain off fat, if needed.

2 Stir in the salsa and sprinkle with cheese. Microwave on high (100% power) for 1 to 2 minutes or until cheese is melted. Meanwhile, combine the sour cream, cilantro, salt, and pepper.

3 Spread sour cream mixture on top of hot bean-meat mixture. Sprinkle with the avocado, tomatoes, and green onions. Serve warm with tortilla chips. Makes 7 cups.

PER TABLESPOON WITH 1 CHIP		DAILY GOAL
Calories	25	2,000 (F), 2,500 (M)
Total fat	2 g	60 g or less (F), 70 g or less (M)
Saturated fat	1 g	20 g or less (F), 23 g or less (M)
Cholesterol	4 mg	300 mg or less
Sodium	50 mg	2,400 mg or less
Carbohydrates	1 g	250 g or more
Protein	1 g	55 g to 90 g

NOTES

_____
_____
_____
_____
_____
_____
_____
_____
_____
_____
_____
_____
_____
_____
_____
_____
_____

LIGHT GUACAMOLE

All the good taste of classic guacamole is preserved in this light version made with nonfat yogurt.

▽ *Low-calorie*
   Prep time: 5 minutes
○ *Degree of difficulty: easy*

1 ripe avocado, peeled and pit removed
2 tablespoons fresh lime juice
½ cup plain nonfat yogurt
1 tablespoon minced red onion
¼ teaspoon salt
¼ teaspoon freshly ground pepper
  Pinch cumin
  Oven-Baked Tortilla Chips
    (recipe, page 31)

Mash the avocado and lime juice with a fork in a small bowl. Stir in the yogurt, red onion, salt, pepper, and cumin. Serve with Oven-Baked Tortilla Chips. Makes 1½ cups.

PER TABLESPOON		DAILY GOAL
Calories	15	2,000 (F), 2,500 (M)
Total fat	1 g	60 g or less (F), 70 g or less (M)
Saturated fat	0 g	20 g or less (F), 23 g or less (M)
Cholesterol	0 mg	300 mg or less
Sodium	27 mg	2,400 mg or less
Carbohydrates	1 g	250 g or more
Protein	0 g	55 g to 90 g

NOTES

_____

_____

_____

_____

_____

_____

_____

_____

_____

_____

_____

_____

_____

_____

_____

_____

_____

_____

GRILLED QUESADILLA

We love the smoky flavor the grill gives this classic Mexican appetizer. *Also pictured on page 56.*

Prep time: 5 minutes
Grilling time: 1 to 2 minutes
O *Degree of difficulty: easy*

8 **flour tortillas**
1 **cup shredded Monterey Jack cheese**
4 **tablespoons chopped fresh cilantro**
   Classic Salsa Cruda
      (recipe, page 29)
   Sour cream and fresh cilantro,
      for garnish (optional)

Prepare grill. Sprinkle each of 4 flour tortillas with ¼ cup of the shredded cheese and 1 tablespoon of the chopped cilantro. Cover with remaining tortillas. Grill over medium-hot coals for 30 to 60 seconds per side or until golden. Spoon Classic Salsa Cruda between tortillas. Cut into wedges and garnish with sour cream and cilantro, if desired. Makes 4 servings.

PER SERVING		DAILY GOAL
Calories	215	2,000 (F), 2,500 (M)
Total fat	10 g	60 g or less (F), 70 g or less (M)
Saturated fat	0 g	20 g or less (F), 23 g or less (M)
Cholesterol	25 mg	300 mg or less
Sodium	233 mg	2,400 mg or less
Carbohydrates	24 g	250 g or more
Protein	10 g	55 g to 90 g

NOTES

YANKEE GRILLED QUESADILLAS

Here's a quesadilla with all the fixings of the beloved grilled cheese sandwich.

Prep time: 10 minutes
Grilling time: 1 to 2 minutes
Degree of difficulty: easy

8 **flour tortillas**
4 **teaspoons butter *or* margarine, melted**
1 **cup shredded cheddar cheese**
4 **slices bacon, cooked and crumbled**
½ **cup diced tomato**

Prepare grill. Brush 1 side of the flour tortillas with the melted butter. Sprinkle the unbuttered side of 4 tortillas evenly with the cheddar, bacon, and tomato. Cover with remaining tortillas, buttered side out. Grill over medium-hot coals for 30 to 60 seconds per side or until golden. Cut into wedges. Makes 4 servings.

PER SERVING		DAILY GOAL
Calories	415	2,000 (F), 2,500 (M)
Total fat	21 g	60 g or less (F), 70 g or less (M)
Saturated fat	10 g	20 g or less (F), 23 g or less (M)
Cholesterol	46 mg	300 mg or less
Sodium	653 mg	2,400 mg or less
Carbohydrates	40 g	250 g or more
Protein	15 g	55 g to 90 g

MICROWAVE CHEESE-CHORIZO DIP

There's simply no substitute for the extra-spicy flavor of chorizo sausage in this quick and delicious three-ingredient dip.

Ⓜ *Microwave*
   Prep time: 10 minutes
   Microwave time: 9 to 11 minutes
Ⓞ *Degree of difficulty: easy*

1 **chorizo sausage (2 ounces), minced**
1 **pound Monterey Jack cheese,**
   shredded (4 cups)
1 **can (4 ounces) chopped green**
   chiles, drained
   Tortilla chips

1 Spread the chorizo between paper towels on a microwave-proof plate. Microwave on high (100% power) about 3 minutes or until browned and crisp.

2 Combine chorizo in a medium bowl with the cheese and chiles. Transfer mixture to a shallow, 3-cup microwave-proof serving dish. Cover with plastic wrap, turning back a section to vent. Microwave on medium (50% power) for 6 to 8 minutes or until cheese is thoroughly melted. Stir quickly and serve with tortilla chips. Makes 6 servings.

PER SERVING		DAILY GOAL
Calories	320	2,000 (F), 2,500 (M)
Total fat	25 g	60 g or less (F), 70 g or less (M)
Saturated fat	14 g	20 g or less (F), 23 g or less (M)
Cholesterol	88 mg	300 mg or less
Sodium	643 mg	2,400 mg or less
Carbohydrates	2 g	250 g or more
Protein	20 g	55 g to 90 g

PEPPER JACK EMPANADAS

These triangles of flaky phyllo filled with three cheeses are delicious served with Light Guacamole (recipe, page 61) and tortilla chips.

Prep time: 1 hour
Baking time: 12 to 15 minutes
Degree of difficulty: moderate

- 1 **package (3 ounces) cream cheese, softened**
- 1½ **cups shredded pepper Jack cheese**
- 1 **cup ricotta cheese**
- ⅓ **cup chopped fresh parsley**
- ½ **cup walnuts, toasted and ground**
- 1 **large egg, lightly beaten**
- 6 **to 8 drops red pepper sauce**
- 20 **sheets phyllo dough**
- ½ **cup butter *or* margarine, melted**

1 Preheat oven to 375°F. Lightly grease 2 cookie sheets. Set aside.

2 Beat the cream cheese in a medium bowl until smooth. Stir in the pepper Jack cheese, ricotta, parsley, walnuts, egg, and pepper sauce until evenly combined.

3 Place 1 phyllo sheet on a work surface and brush lightly with butter. Top with a second phyllo sheet and brush with butter. With a sharp knife, cut crosswise into five 3-inch-wide strips. Place 1 rounded teaspoon cheese mixture on the end of each strip. Fold up around filling to form a triangle (flag-style). Transfer triangles, seam side down, to prepared cookie sheets and brush tops lightly with butter. Repeat with remaining phyllo, butter, and filling. (Can be made ahead. Freeze on cookie sheets. Transfer to freezer-proof plastic bags and store up to 1 month.)

4 Bake for 12 to 15 minutes (20 to 25 minutes, if frozen) or until lightly golden. Serve warm. Makes 50 appetizers.

PER APPETIZER		DAILY GOAL
Calories	75	2,000 (F), 2,500 (M)
Total fat	6 g	60 g or less (F), 70 g or less (M)
Saturated fat	3 g	20 g or less (F), 23 g or less (M)
Cholesterol	17 mg	300 mg or less
Sodium	82 mg	2,400 mg or less
Carbohydrates	4 g	250 g or more
Protein	2 g	55 g to 90 g

NOTES

_____

_____

_____

_____

_____

_____

_____

_____

_____

_____

_____

_____

JICAMA WITH CHILI DIP

Toasting the chili powder mellows the raw, burning taste. Any leftover chili salt keeps indefinitely.

▼ *Low-fat*
▽ *Low-calorie*
   Prep time: 10 minutes
○ *Degree of difficulty: easy*

2 tablespoons chili powder
1 tablespoon salt
3 tablespoons fresh lemon juice
   Cold water
2 large or 4 small jicamas

1 Place the chili powder in a small skillet. Toast chili powder, stirring constantly, over medium heat about 1 minute or until fragrant. Stir in the salt. Transfer mixture to a tiny serving bowl or saucer.

2 Stir the lemon juice into a large bowl of cold water. Peel the jicama. Cut jicama into thin sticks or wedges and drop into the lemon juice-water mixture.

3 To serve, drain jicama, then pat dry on paper towels and arrange on a plate. Serve with chili-salt mixture for dipping. Makes 12 servings.

PER SERVING		DAILY GOAL
Calories	35	2,000 (F), 2,500 (M)
Total fat	0 g	60 g or less (F), 70 g or less (M)
Saturated fat	0 g	20 g or less (F), 23 g or less (M)
Cholesterol	0 mg	300 mg or less
Sodium	566 mg	2,400 mg or less
Carbohydrates	7 g	250 g or more
Protein	1 g	55 g to 90 g

NO-GUILT NACHOS

With our Oven-Baked Tortilla Chips (recipe, page 31) and our lean refried beans, you'll find these crunchy nachos just as delicious as the high fat kind.

▼ *Low-fat*
Prep time: 20 minutes
Cooking time: 8 to 12 minutes
○ *Degree of difficulty: easy*

2 **teaspoons vegetable oil**
⅓ **cup finely chopped onion**
1 **teaspoon minced garlic**
½ **teaspoon cumin**
⅛ **teaspoon ground red pepper**
1 **can (15 ounces) pinto beans,**
      drained and rinsed
¼ **cup warm water**
2 **teaspoons fresh lemon *or* lime**
      juice
   Oven-Baked Tortilla Chips
      (recipe, page 31)
½ **cup shredded low-fat cheddar**
      cheese
   Classic Salsa Cruda
      (recipe, page 29)

1 Preheat oven to 350°F. Heat the oil in a medium saucepan over medium heat. Add the onion and cook about 3 minutes or until softened. Stir in the garlic, cumin, and red pepper and cook about 30 seconds or until fragrant. Add the beans and cook 1 minute more, mashing beans with a spoon. Stir in the water and cook until water is absorbed. Remove from heat and stir in the lemon juice.

2 Spread the Oven-Baked Tortilla Chips on an oven-proof plate or pie plate. Top with bean mixture and sprinkle with the cheese. Bake for 3 to 5 minutes or until cheese is melted. Top with Classic Salsa Cruda. Makes 4 servings.

PER SERVING		DAILY GOAL
Calories	250	2,000 (F), 2,500 (M)
Total fat	6 g	60 g or less (F), 70 g or less (M)
Saturated fat	2 g	20 g or less (F), 23 g or less (M)
Cholesterol	10 mg	300 mg or less
Sodium	353 mg	2,400 mg or less
Carbohydrates	35 g	250 g or more
Protein	11 g	55 g to 90 g

NOTES

KOREAN BARBECUED MEATBALLS

Serve these fragrant beef skewers with chunks of fresh pineapple and papaya.

Prep time: 30 minutes plus chilling
Grilling time: 10 to 12 minutes
○ *Degree of difficulty: easy*

1	**pound lean ground beef**
⅓	**cup minced green onions**
¼	**cup chopped onion**
3	**tablespoons soy sauce**
2	**tablespoons sesame seeds, toasted**
1	**tablespoon granulated sugar**
1	**tablespoon vegetable oil**

1 Combine the beef, green onions, chopped onion, soy sauce, sesame seeds, sugar, and oil in a medium bowl. Shape meat mixture into 1-inch balls. Transfer meatballs to a jelly-roll pan; cover and refrigerate for 1 hour.

2 Meanwhile, soak 20 wooden skewers in water for 30 minutes. Prepare grill or preheat broiler. Thread 2 meatballs on each skewer, then grill over medium coals for 5 to 6 minutes per side or until meatballs are cooked through. Serve immediately. Makes 20 appetizers.

PER APPETIZER		DAILY GOAL
Calories	60	2,000 (F), 2,500 (M)
Total fat	4 g	60 g or less (F), 70 g or less (M)
Saturated fat	1 g	20 g or less (F), 23 g or less (M)
Cholesterol	4 mg	300 mg or less
Sodium	167 mg	2,400 mg or less
Carbohydrates	1 g	250 g or more
Protein	4 g	55 g to 90 g

NOTES

ZESTY BACON AND HORSERADISH DIP

Here's a sour cream dip with plenty of zip tailor-made for football season.

Prep time: 15 minutes plus chilling
Cooking time: 8 minutes
O *Degree of difficulty: easy*

6   slices bacon
1   small onion, finely chopped
1   garlic clove, minced
1   package (3 ounces) cream cheese, softened
1   cup sour cream
1   tablespoon prepared horseradish
1   teaspoon Dijon mustard
½   teaspoon freshly ground pepper
¼   teaspoon salt
    Assorted raw vegetables and crackers

1 Cook the bacon in a medium skillet until crisp, then transfer to paper towels and drain.

2 Pour off all but 1 tablespoon of drippings from skillet. Add the onion and garlic and cook over medium heat about 3 minutes or until tender. Crumble bacon into a medium bowl and add onion mixture. Stir in the cream cheese, sour cream, horseradish, mustard, pepper, and salt until blended. Cover and refrigerate for 2 hours or overnight.

3 Remove dip from refrigerator and let stand at room temperature 1 hour before serving. Serve with vegetables and crackers. Makes 1¼ cups.

PER TABLESPOON		DAILY GOAL
Calories	60	2,000 (F), 2,500 (M)
Total fat	5 g	60 g or less (F), 70 g or less (M)
Saturated fat	3 g	20 g or less (F), 23 g or less (M)
Cholesterol	12 mg	300 mg or less
Sodium	86 mg	2,400 mg or less
Carbohydrates	1 g	250 g or more
Protein	1 g	55 g to 90 g

BUFFALO CHICKEN WINGS

First served in a neighborhood bar in Buffalo, New York, these tasty morsels have become one of America's favorite finger foods.

Prep time: 20 minutes plus chilling
Baking time: 45 minutes
○ *Degree of difficulty: easy*

Dip
- ½ **cup sour cream**
- ½ **cup mayonnaise**
- 2 **ounces blue cheese, crumbled**
- 1 **green onion, thinly sliced**
- ½ **teaspoon minced garlic**
- ¼ **teaspoon salt**
- ¼ **teaspoon freshly ground pepper**

Wings
- 24 **chicken wings (about 4 pounds)**
- 2 **tablespoons butter *or* margarine, melted**
- 4 **to 5 tablespoons Louisiana hot sauce**
- 2 **teaspoons cider vinegar**
  Celery sticks

1 For dip, combine the sour cream, mayonnaise, blue cheese, green onion, garlic, salt, and pepper in a medium bowl. Cover and refrigerate at least 1 hour.

2 Preheat oven to 450°F. Arrange the wings on a flat rack in a roasting pan.

3 Combine the butter, hot sauce, and vinegar in a small bowl. Brush half the sauce on the wings and bake for 25 minutes. Turn wings. Brush remaining sauce on wings and bake about 20 minutes more or until golden and crisp. Serve with dip and celery sticks. Makes 8 servings.

PER SERVING		DAILY GOAL
Calories	430	2,000 (F), 2,500 (M)
Total fat	35 g	60 g or less (F), 70 g or less (M)
Saturated fat	11 g	20 g or less (F), 23 g or less (M)
Cholesterol	99 mg	300 mg or less
Sodium	573 mg	2,400 mg or less
Carbohydrates	1 g	250 g or more
Protein	25 g	55 g to 90 g

NOTES

CHEESE WAFERS

There are many cheesy crackers on the market, but nothing beats the rich and buttery flavor of these homemade wafers. We've prepared half with nuts and half without—either way, they're delicious.

Prep time: 30 minutes plus chilling
Baking time: 20 to 24 minutes
○ *Degree of difficulty: easy*

1   **cup butter *or* margarine, softened**
2   **cups shredded sharp cheddar cheese**
2   **teaspoons Worcestershire sauce**
2   **cups all-purpose flour**
½   **teaspoon salt**
¼   **teaspoon ground red pepper**
2   **large egg yolks**
2   **tablespoons milk**
½   **cup finely chopped walnuts**

1 Beat the butter and cheese in a large mixing bowl until light, then beat in the Worcestershire sauce. On low speed, beat in the flour, salt, and red pepper until well mixed. Divide dough into quarters. Shape each quarter into a log, 1 inch in diameter. Wrap logs in wax paper and refrigerate at least 3 hours or overnight.

2 Preheat oven to 375°F. Whisk together the egg yolks and milk in a small bowl. Cut 2 logs into ¼-inch-thick slices. Arrange on 2 ungreased cookie sheets and brush tops with beaten egg mixture. Sprinkle with nuts. Bake for 10 to 12 minutes or until golden. Transfer to wire racks and cool. Repeat process with remaining logs, omitting the nuts. (Can be made ahead. Freeze wafers in an airtight container up to 1 month. Thaw at room temperature.) Makes about 12 dozen wafers.

PER WAFER		DAILY GOAL
Calories	30	2,000 (F), 2,500 (M)
Total fat	2 g	60 g or less (F), 70 g or less (M)
Saturated fat	1 g	20 g or less (F), 23 g or less (M)
Cholesterol	8 mg	300 mg or less
Sodium	31 mg	2,400 mg or less
Carbohydrates	1 g	250 g or more
Protein	1 g	55 g to 90 g

NOTES

WINE BISCUITS

Crisp and peppery, these bite-size nibblers are a wonderful accompaniment to a glass of wine.

Prep time: 20 minutes plus cooling and chilling
Baking time: 12 minutes per batch
○ *Degree of difficulty: easy*

1   cup dry white wine
2   cups all-purpose flour
1   teaspoon baking powder
     Freshly ground pepper
½   teaspoon salt
½   cup butter, softened
        (no substitutions)
¼   cup vegetable shortening
½   cup granulated sugar
1   large egg white, beaten with
        1 tablespoon water

1 Bring the wine to a boil in a small saucepan over high heat. Boil for 8 to 10 minutes or until reduced to ¼ cup. Cool to room temperature.

2 Combine the flour, baking powder, ¾ teaspoon pepper, and the salt in a medium bowl. Beat the butter, shortening, and sugar in a large mixing bowl until light and fluffy. Blend in cooled wine. Add dry ingredients and beat 1 minute. (Dough will be sticky.) Divide dough in half. Spoon each half onto a sheet of plastic wrap and shape each into 10x1-inch log. Wrap and freeze overnight.

3 Preheat oven to 350°F. Cut chilled logs into ¼-inch-thick slices. Place slices 1 inch apart on 2 ungreased cookie sheets. Brush tops of biscuits with the beaten egg white. Grind additional pepper on top.

4 Bake about 12 minutes or until edges are golden, switching position of cookie sheets halfway through baking. Cool biscuits completely on cookie sheets. (Can be made ahead. Transfer biscuits to an airtight container and store at room temperature up to 1 month.) Makes about 80 biscuits.

PER BISCUIT		DAILY GOAL
Calories	30	2,000 (F), 2,500 (M)
Total fat	2 g	60 g or less (F), 70 g or less (M)
Saturated fat	1 g	20 g or less (F), 23 g or less (M)
Cholesterol	3 mg	300 mg or less
Sodium	32 mg	2,400 mg or less
Carbohydrates	4 g	250 g or more
Protein	0 g	55 g to 90 g

NOTES

CLASSIC ONION RINGS

These golden rings are positively addictive! For the crispiest results when frying be sure to reheat the oil between batches.

Prep time: 15 minutes
Cooking time: 3 minutes per batch
○ *Degree of difficulty: easy*

- 1 **large sweet onion (1¼ pounds)**
- ½ **cup milk**
- 1½ **cups all-purpose flour**
   Salt
- ⅛ **teaspoon freshly ground pepper**
   Vegetable oil, for frying

1 Slice the onion into ¼-inch-thick slices, then separate slices into rings. Toss rings with the milk in a large bowl. Combine the flour, ¾ teaspoon salt, and pepper in a medium bowl.

2 Heat 2 inches of the oil to 375°F. in a heavy, large pot or deep-fryer.

3 Drain onions, reserving milk. Dip rings, a few at a time, in flour mixture. Dip in reserved milk, then again in flour. Carefully transfer a few rings to hot oil and fry about 3 minutes or until golden brown. Remove rings with a slotted spoon; drain on paper towels and sprinkle with additional salt. Repeat dipping and frying remaining onion rings, allowing the oil to return to 375°F. between batches. Makes about 3 dozen rings.

PER RING		DAILY GOAL
Calories	50	2,000 (F), 2,500 (M)
Total fat	2 g	60 g or less (F), 70 g or less (M)
Saturated fat	0 g	20 g or less (F), 23 g or less (M)
Cholesterol	0 mg	300 mg or less
Sodium	49 mg	2,400 mg or less
Carbohydrates	6 g	250 g or more
Protein	1 g	55 g to 90 g

THE WAY TO DEEP FRY

Many of our appetizers are deep fried, which requires a heavy Dutch oven or deep-fat fryer filled with 3 to 4 cups of vegetable oil. *(Do not use butter or olive oil.)*

Be sure to allow time to heat your oil to the proper temperature, about 375°F. If you don't have a deep-fat thermometer, drop a cube of white bread into the heated oil. Bubbles should immediately appear around the bread and it should brown within 60 seconds. If the oil is not hot enough, your food will absorb too much oil and become greasy.

A good rule of thumb is to fry your nibbles in small batches so the pan never gets crowded and the oil does not cool down. Turn the food constantly with a large, metal slotted spoon or spatula and fry until evenly golden. Transfer the bites to a jelly-roll pan lined with paper towels and keep them warm in a low oven.

Deep-fried appetizers are best served immediately, while they are still piping hot and crisp.

FRIED MOZZARELLA WITH ANCHOVY DIP

Mini grilled cheese sandwiches for the sophisticate.

Prep time: 25 minutes
Cooking time: 2 minutes per batch
O *Degree of difficulty: easy*

Dip

2   tablespoons butter *or* margarine
1   can (2 ounces) flat anchovies, drained and chopped
1   teaspoon minced garlic
1   tablespoon capers, drained and chopped
1   tablespoon chopped fresh parsley

Mozzarella

6   tablespoons butter *or* margarine, softened
2   tablespoons chopped fresh parsley
½   teaspoon grated lemon peel
20   slices very thinly sliced white bread, crusts trimmed
1   pound mozzarella cheese, very thinly sliced

1 For dip, melt the butter in a small skillet over low heat, then add the anchovies, garlic, capers, and parsley. Cook until heated through. Set aside. Makes ⅓ cup.

2 For mozzarella, combine the butter, parsley, and lemon peel in a small bowl. Spread the mixture evenly over 1 side of the bread slices. Arrange the mozzarella on the unbuttered sides of 10 slices of bread, then top with remaining slices, buttered side out.

3 Heat a large nonstick skillet over medium heat. Cook sandwiches in batches about 1 minute per side or until golden brown. Transfer sandwiches to a cutting board and cut each sandwich into 4 triangles. (Can be made ahead. Cool sandwiches, then transfer to cookie sheets. Cover with plastic wrap and refrigerate up to 24 hours. Uncover and reheat in a preheated 350°F. oven 4 to 5 minutes.) Transfer to a serving plate. Reheat dip until warm and serve with sandwiches. Makes about 40 appetizers.

PER APPETIZER		DAILY GOAL
Calories	80	2,000 (F), 2,500 (M)
Total fat	5 g	60 g or less (F), 70 g or less (M)
Saturated fat	3 g	20 g or less (F), 23 g or less (M)
Cholesterol	16 mg	300 mg or less
Sodium	161 mg	2,400 mg or less
Carbohydrates	5 g	250 g or more
Protein	3 g	55 g to 90 g

NOTES

FRIED CALAMARI WITH CREAMY SALSA

Here's the super crispy calamari we all love with a new dipping sauce. You control the heat simply by using mild or hot prepared salsa.

Prep time: 20 minutes plus chilling
Cooking time: 1 minute per batch
Degree of difficulty: moderate

Creamy Salsa
- ½ cup mayonnaise
- 3 tablespoons prepared salsa
- 2 teaspoons minced pickled jalapeño chile
- 1 teaspoon jalapeño chile pickle liquid

Calamari
- 1 pound cleaned squid
- ¼ cup all-purpose flour
- ¼ cup cornstarch
  Salt
- ¼ teaspoon freshly ground pepper
- ¼ cup beer
- 2 tablespoons butter *or* margarine, melted
- 1 large egg yolk
- ¼ teaspoon hot pepper sauce
  Vegetable oil, for frying

1 For Creamy Salsa, combine the mayonnaise, salsa, minced jalapeño, and jalapeño liquid in a medium bowl until smooth. Cover and refrigerate until ready to serve.

2 Slice the squid bodies into ½-inch-thick rings, keeping tentacles intact. Combine the flour, cornstarch, ¼ teaspoon salt, and the pepper in a large bowl. Whisk in the beer, butter, egg yolk, and hot pepper sauce until smooth.

3 Heat 1½ inches of oil in a large deep pot or Dutch oven to 375°F. on a frying thermometer. Dip squid into batter, then add to pot with a slotted spoon a few pieces at a time. Cook squid about 1 minute or until golden. Transfer with slotted spoon to paper towels to drain. Sprinkle lightly with salt. Repeat process with remaining squid. Transfer to a serving platter and serve immediately with Creamy Salsa. Makes 6 servings.

PER SERVING		DAILY GOAL
Calories	370	2,000 (F), 2,500 (M)
Total fat	29 g	60 g or less (F), 70 g or less (M)
Saturated fat	6 g	20 g or less (F), 23 g or less (M)
Cholesterol	232 mg	300 mg or less
Sodium	375 mg	2,400 mg or less
Carbohydrates	13 g	250 g or more
Protein	13 g	55 g to 90 g

NOTES

SWEET AND SASSY CASHEWS

Let your microwave go nuts! We think cashews are worth the splurge here, but this spicy coating works well with peanuts, too.

Ⓜ *Microwave*
Prep time: 5 minutes
Microwave time: 4 to 6 minutes
○ *Degree of difficulty: easy*

2 **cups roasted cashews**
1 **large egg white, lightly beaten**
½ **cup granulated sugar**
1 **teaspoon ginger**
½ **teaspoon ground red pepper**

1 Lightly oil a jelly-roll pan. Toss the nuts with the egg white in a large microwave-proof bowl until coated. Combine the sugar, ginger, and red pepper in a cup, then stir into nut mixture.

2 Microwave on high (100% power) for 4 to 6 minutes, stirring after 3 minutes, or until caramelized. Spread in the prepared pan and cool. Separate into small pieces. Makes 2 cups.

PER TABLESPOON		DAILY GOAL
Calories	60	2,000 (F), 2,500 (M)
Total fat	4 g	60 g or less (F), 70 g or less (M)
Saturated fat	1 g	20 g or less (F), 23 g or less (M)
Cholesterol	0 mg	300 mg or less
Sodium	3 mg	2,400 mg or less
Carbohydrates	5 g	250 g or more
Protein	1 g	55 g to 90 g

NOTES

SPICY HONEY-ROASTED PEANUTS

These nuts are slow-roasted to perfection. Raw, skinned peanuts are available at most health food stores.

Prep time: 5 minutes
Baking time: 25 minutes
O *Degree of difficulty: easy*

2 **tablespoons butter *or* margarine, melted**
2 **tablespoons honey**
2 **teaspoons minced garlic**
1 **teaspoon ground red pepper**
1 **teaspoon ginger**
1 **teaspoon salt**
1 **pound raw, skinned peanuts**

1 Preheat oven to 325°F. Combine the butter, honey, garlic, red pepper, ginger, and salt in a medium bowl. Stir in the peanuts until well coated.

2 Spread nuts in a shallow baking pan and roast about 25 minutes or until toasted and fragrant, stirring once or twice. Cool. (Can be made ahead. Store in an airtight container at room temperature up to 1 week.) Makes 3 cups.

PER TABLESPOON		DAILY GOAL
Calories	60	2,000 (F), 2,500 (M)
Total fat	5 g	60 g or less (F), 70 g or less (M)
Saturated fat	1 g	20 g or less (F), 23 g or less (M)
Cholesterol	1 mg	300 mg or less
Sodium	52 mg	2,400 mg or less
Carbohydrates	2 g	250 g or more
Protein	2 g	55 g to 90 g

PERFECT

PARTY FOOD

When it's time to get festive, nothing gets things going like this selection of party-pleasing appetizers. You'll find morsels of finger food all wrapped up and ready for passing— Moroccan Triangles, Samosas with Yogurt Sauce, and Cheese and Artichoke Crescents. Or, if a buffet table is more your style, try a sampling including Smoked Salmon Ribbon Sandwiches, Quiche Lorraine Squares, Swedish Meatballs, and Snapper Paté.

SAMOSAS WITH YOGURT SAUCE

Prep time: 1½ hours
Baking time: 17 to 20 minutes per batch
● *Degree of difficulty: moderate*

Pastry

- 3 cups all-purpose flour
- ¼ teaspoon salt
- ¼ teaspoon ground red pepper
- ¾ cup vegetable shortening
- 7 to 10 tablespoons ice water

Filling

- ¾ pound baking potatoes, peeled and chopped
- Salt
- Water
- 2 tablespoons vegetable oil, divided
- ½ cup minced onion
- 2 teaspoons minced garlic
- 1 teaspoon minced ginger
- 4 teaspoons minced jalapeño chiles
- 1 teaspoon curry powder
- ½ teaspoon cumin
- ⅛ teaspoon ground red pepper
- ⅓ cup frozen baby peas, thawed

- 1 tablespoon minced fresh cilantro
- 1 large egg, lightly beaten

Sauce

- 1 container (16 ounces) plain low-fat yogurt
- 2 tablespoons minced fresh cilantro
- 2 tablespoons minced fresh mint
- ½ teaspoon cumin
- ½ teaspoon salt
- ¼ teaspoon freshly ground pepper

1 For pastry, combine the flour, salt, and ground red pepper in a large bowl. Cut in shortening until mixture resembles fine crumbs. Sprinkle with ice water, 1 tablespoon at a time, tossing with a fork until pastry holds together. Shape into a disk; wrap and chill while preparing filling.

2 Meanwhile, for filling, bring potatoes, 1 teaspoon salt, and enough cold water to cover to a boil in a small saucepan. Boil 12 to 15 minutes or until tender. Drain, then transfer to a medium bowl and mash coarsely with a spoon. Set aside.

3 Heat 1 tablespoon of the oil in a large nonstick skillet over medium heat. Add onion, garlic, and ginger; cook 4 minutes or until vegetables are tender. Add jalapeño, curry, cumin, ¾ teaspoon salt,

and red pepper; cook 30 seconds or until fragrant. Stir in mashed potatoes, peas, cilantro, and remaining 1 tablespoon oil.

4 Preheat oven to 400°F. Grease 2 cookie sheets. Set aside. Divide dough into quarters. On a lightly floured surface, roll one quarter of pastry (keeping remaining dough refrigerated) very thin, about ¹⁄₁₆-inch thick. Cut circles with a floured, 2½-inch round cutter. Place a level teaspoon of filling onto half of each pastry circle. Brush edge of pastry with water and fold over filling, then press edges of pastry with a fork to seal. Arrange pastries 1 inch apart on a prepared cookie sheet. Combine the egg and 1 teaspoon water in a cup and brush over pastries. Repeat with remaining pastry, filling, and egg mixture, rerolling scraps.

5 Bake pastries, 1 cookie sheet at a time, 17 to 20 minutes or until golden. Transfer to wire racks; cool slightly. (Can be made ahead. Cool completely. Freeze in a single layer on jelly-roll pans. To reheat, cover frozen pastries with foil and place in a preheated 375°F. oven for 15 minutes.)

6 For sauce, combine the yogurt, cilantro, mint, cumin, salt, and pepper in a small bowl. Serve with warm pastries. Makes 60 appetizers.

QUICHE LORRAINE SQUARES

We've taken this classic cheese pie from the Lorraine region in France and made it into elegant bite-size squares. Serve these savory morsels warm or at room temperature.

Prep time: 25 minutes plus chilling
Baking time: 43 to 50 minutes
● *Degree of difficulty: moderate*

Pastry

- 2 cups all-purpose flour
- 1 teaspoon salt
- ½ cup vegetable shortening
- ¼ cup cold butter *or* margarine, cut up
- 5 to 6 tablespoons cold water

Filling

- 2 slices bacon
- 1 cup chopped onions
- 8 large eggs
- 2 cups half-and-half *or* light cream
- ¼ teaspoon freshly ground pepper
  Pinch nutmeg
- 8 ounces gruyère *or* Swiss cheese, shredded (2 cups)

1 For pastry, place the flour and salt in a large bowl. Cut in the shortening and butter until mixture resembles coarse crumbs. Sprinkle with water, 1 tablespoon at a time, tossing with a fork until pastry holds together.

2 On a lightly floured surface with a floured rolling pin, roll dough into a rectangle, 2 inches larger all around than a 15½ x10½-inch jelly-roll pan. Fold dough into quarters and gently ease into pan, allowing dough to overhang edge. (If pastry tears, press together with fingertips.) Fold overhang in and press into side of the pan, then trim the pastry even with the edge of the pan. Freeze about 15 minutes or until firm.

3 Meanwhile, preheat oven to 425°F. Line pastry with foil and fill with dried beans or uncooked rice. Bake for 15 minutes. Remove foil and beans, then bake for 8 to 10 minutes more or until pastry is golden brown. Cool on a wire rack. Reduce oven temperature to 350°F.

4 For filling, cook the bacon in a medium skillet over medium heat until crisp. Remove bacon with a slotted spoon and transfer to paper towels to drain. Crumble bacon. Add the onions to drippings in skillet and cook for 6 to 8 minutes or until tender and lightly browned.

5 Whisk the eggs in a medium bowl with the cream, pepper, and nutmeg until blended. Sprinkle bacon, cheese, and onions over crust, then pour egg mixture over filling. Bake for 20 to 25 minutes or until filling is just set in center. Cool 15 minutes. Cut into 1½-inch squares. (Can be made ahead. Cover and refrigerate overnight. Uncover and reheat in a preheated 350°F. oven 10 to 15 minutes.) Makes 54 appetizers.

MUSHROOM TARTLETS

We've combined two types of mushrooms to create a filling with great flavor. *Also pictured on page 82.*

Prep time: 1 hour
Baking time: 8 to 10 minutes per batch
 *Degree of difficulty: moderate*

Toast Cups
3 tablespoons butter, melted (no substitutions)
2 loaves very thinly sliced white bread

Filling
¼ cup dried porcini mushrooms
¼ cup boiling water
2 tablespoons butter
1 tablespoon minced shallot
¾ pound fresh mushrooms, finely chopped
1 tablespoon cornstarch
¼ cup heavy *or* whipping cream
1 tablespoon brandy
½ teaspoon salt
¼ teaspoon freshly ground pepper
½ cup diced plum tomato
1 tablespoon chopped fresh flat-leaf parsley
Flat-leaf parsley

1 Preheat oven to 350°F. For toast cups, brush 2 mini muffin pan cups with some of the melted butter. With a rolling pin, roll the bread slices thin, then cut into 2½-inch squares. Press into prepared muffin pans. Bake for 8 to 10 minutes or until golden. Repeat with the remaining butter and bread. (Can be made ahead. Store in airtight containers up to 2 days.)

2 For filling, soak the porcini mushrooms in boiling water in a small bowl. Melt the butter in a medium saucepan over medium heat, then add the shallot and cook 2 minutes. Remove porcini mushrooms from liquid with a slotted spoon and chop fine. Add to the saucepan with the fresh mushrooms and cook, stirring, 7 minutes. Whisk together the cornstarch and cream in a small bowl, then stir into mushrooms. Add the brandy, salt, and pepper, then boil, stirring, 2 minutes. Stir in the tomato and parsley.

3 Spoon filling by slightly rounded teaspoonfuls into toast cups. Garnish with parsley. Serve immediately. (Can be made ahead. Let stand at room temperature 1 hour. Reheat in a preheated 400°F. oven 5 minutes.) Makes 4 dozen appetizers.

PER APPETIZER		DAILY GOAL
Calories	35	2,000 (F), 2,500 (M)
Total fat	2 g	60 g or less (F), 70 g or less (M)
Saturated fat	1 g	20 g or less (F), 23 g or less (M)
Cholesterol	5 mg	300 mg or less
Sodium	81 mg	2,400 mg or less
Carbohydrates	5 g	250 g or more
Protein	1 g	55 g to 90 g

NOTES

_____

_____

_____

_____

_____

_____

_____

_____

_____

MOROCCAN TRIANGLES

We used yogurt instead of sour cream to reduce the fat in the dipping sauce for these light-as-air appetizers.

Ⓜ *Microwave*
Prep time: 50 minutes plus standing
Baking time: 10 minutes
◗ *Degree of difficulty: moderate*

Dip
1 **container (16 ounces) low-fat yogurt**
¼ **teaspoon ground coriander**
Pinch salt

Filling
1 **large baking potato**
1 **teaspoon dried mint**
1 **tablespoon fresh lemon juice**
2 **teaspoons olive oil**
1 **cup finely chopped onions**
2 **teaspoons minced garlic**
1 **teaspoon cumin**
¼ **teaspoon freshly ground pepper**
⅛ **teaspoon ground red pepper**
1 **package (10 ounces) frozen chopped spinach, thawed and squeezed dry**
¾ **teaspoon salt**
⅓ **cup chopped flat leaf parsley**

8 **sheets phyllo dough**
3 **to 4 tablespoons olive oil**

1 For dip, line a sieve with a coffee filter. Spoon in the yogurt and let drain 1 hour. Transfer drained yogurt to a medium bowl and discard liquid. Stir in the coriander and a pinch of salt.

2 Meanwhile, for filling, rinse the potato and prick all over with a fork; wrap in wax paper. Microwave on high (100% power) about 6 minutes or until tender, turning once. Let potato stand for 5 minutes, then peel and chop.

3 Preheat oven to 400°F. Sprinkle the mint over the lemon juice in a large bowl and set aside. Heat the oil in a large skillet over medium heat. Add the onions and cook, stirring, for 5 to 8 minutes or until tender. Stir in the garlic, cumin, and both peppers and cook 30 seconds or until fragrant. Stir in the spinach and ¾ teaspoon salt and cook 1 minute more. Add to bowl with mint-lemon mixture and stir in the potato and parsley.

4 Place 1 sheet of phyllo dough on a work surface and brush lightly with some of the oil. (Keep remaining phyllo covered.) Top with a second phyllo sheet and brush lightly with oil. Cut phyllo lengthwise into 4 equal strips. Place 1 generous tablespoon filling on end of each strip and fold up to form triangles. Transfer packets to an ungreased cookie sheet and brush lightly with oil. Repeat with remaining phyllo, oil, and filling to make 16 packets. Bake 10 minutes or until golden. (Can be made ahead. Cool. Wrap well and refrigerate up to 24 hours. Reheat in preheated 400°F. oven 5 to 10 minutes.) Serve hot with dip. Makes 16 appetizers.

PER APPETIZER		DAILY GOAL
Calories	90	2,000 (F), 2,500 (M)
Total fat	4 g	60 g or less (F), 70 g or less (M)
Saturated fat	1 g	20 g or less (F), 23 g or less (M)
Cholesterol	1 mg	300 mg or less
Sodium	177 mg	2,400 mg or less
Carbohydrates	11 g	250 g or more
Protein	3 g	55 g to 90 g

CORNMEAL-BUTTERMILK BISCUITS

These are fabulous split and served with your favorite baked ham. If you're short on time, order a precooked ham and have it sliced by the butcher.

Prep time: 25 minutes
Baking time: 10 minutes
O *Degree of difficulty: easy*

- 3 cups all-purpose flour
- 1 cup yellow cornmeal
- 4 teaspoons baking powder
- 2 teaspoons granulated sugar
- 1 teaspoon baking soda
- 1 teaspoon salt
- ¼ teaspoon ground red pepper
- ⅔ cup cold butter *or* margarine, cut up
- 1½ cups buttermilk
- 1 large egg, beaten
- 3 tablespoons butter *or* margarine, melted
- Baked ham, sliced

1 Preheat oven to 450°F. Grease 2 cookie sheets. Set aside.

2 Combine the flour, cornmeal, baking powder, sugar, baking soda, salt, and red pepper in a large bowl. With a pastry blender or 2 knives, cut in butter until mixture resembles coarse crumbs. Stir in the buttermilk just until combined.

3 On a lightly floured surface with a floured rolling pin, roll the dough ½-inch thick. Cut into circles with a floured, 2-inch round cookie cutter, rerolling and cutting scraps. Transfer biscuits to prepared cookie sheets and brush the tops with beaten egg. Bake about 10 minutes or until golden. Transfer to wire racks to cool slightly. (Can be made ahead. Cool completely. Wrap and freeze up to 1 month. Thaw covered at room temperature. Uncover and reheat in batches in a preheated 400°F. oven 5 minutes.) Split biscuits and brush cut sides with melted butter. Serve with baked ham. Makes about 40 biscuits.

PER BISCUIT		DAILY GOAL
Calories	90	2,000 (F), 2,500 (M)
Total fat	4 g	60 g or less (F), 70 g or less (M)
Saturated fat	3 g	20 g or less (F), 23 g or less (M)
Cholesterol	16 mg	300 mg or less
Sodium	187 mg	2,400 mg or less
Carbohydrates	11 g	250 g or more
Protein	2 g	55 g to 90 g

NOTES

ZUCCHINI FRITTERS WITH CORIANDER CHUTNEY

Spice it up! Our Indian-style chutney is a tangy purée of cilantro (coriander's other name), lime, and chile.

Prep time: 35 minutes
Cooking time: 2 to 3 minutes per batch
◑ *Degree of difficulty: moderate*

Chutney
- 1 **poblano chile** *or* **green pepper**
- 1 **cup fresh cilantro leaves**
- ½ **cup fresh parsley leaves**
- 2 **tablespoons vegetable oil**
  Pinch ground red pepper
- 1 **tablespoon fresh lime juice**
- ½ **teaspoon salt**

Fritters
- 2 **medium zucchini (8 ounces)**
- 1 **large egg, divided**
- ¼ **cup milk**
- ¼ **cup shredded pepper Jack cheese**
- 1 **green onion, sliced**
- ¾ **cup all-purpose flour**
- ½ **teaspoon baking powder**
- ½ **teaspoon cumin**
- ½ **teaspoon salt**
  Vegetable oil, for frying

1 For chutney, roast the poblano chile directly on a gas or electric burner over medium-high heat until evenly charred. Place in a brown paper bag; fold over and cool.

2 When chile is cool enough to handle, peel and remove stem and seeds. Place the chile, cilantro, parsley, oil, red pepper, lime juice, and salt in a blender. Blend until smooth. Set aside.

3 For fritters, shred 2 cups of zucchini on the coarse side of a grater onto several layers of paper towels. Whisk the egg yolk, milk, cheese, and green onion in a medium bowl. Pat zucchini dry and add to yolk mixture. Beat the egg white to stiff peaks in a small mixing bowl.

4 Combine the flour, baking powder, cumin, and salt in a small bowl. Stir into zucchini mixture, then fold in egg white with a rubber spatula just until mixed.

5 Meanwhile, heat 1½ inches of oil in a heavy saucepan or electric skillet to 375°F. Carefully drop batter by teaspoonfuls, 4 at a time, into hot oil. Cook, turning once, for 2 to 3 minutes or until golden. Drain on paper towels. Serve with chutney. Makes about 2 dozen fritters.

PER FRITTER WITH 1 TEASPOON CHUTNEY		DAILY GOAL
Calories	60	2,000 (F), 2,500 (M)
Total fat	4 g	60 g or less (F), 70 g or less (M)
Saturated fat	1 g	20 g or less (F), 23 g or less (M)
Cholesterol	10 mg	300 mg or less
Sodium	114 mg	2,400 mg or less
Carbohydrates	4 g	250 g or more
Protein	1 g	55 g to 90 g

NOTES

_____

_____

_____

_____

_____

_____

_____

_____

LUSCIOUS
LIME SHRIMP

For a quick and easy appetizer, try a blend of fragrant cilantro and citrusy tartness, served on cucumber slices.

▼   *Low-fat*
▽   *Low-calorie*
     Prep time: 35 minutes plus standing
     Broiling time: 3 minutes
○   *Degree of difficulty: easy*

  3 **tablespoons fresh lime juice**
  1 **green onion, chopped**
  2 **tablespoons chopped fresh cilantro**
  1 **teaspoon minced jalapeño chile**
  1 **teaspoon olive oil**
  ½ **teaspoon minced garlic**
  ⅛ **teaspoon salt**
 20 **large shrimp (about 1 pound),**
     peeled and deveined
  1 **tablespoon minced red pepper**
 20 **cucumber slices**

1 Stir together the lime juice, green onion, cilantro, jalapeño, oil, garlic, and salt in a medium bowl. Toss the shrimp with 2 tablespoons of the dressing in another medium bowl. Cover and refrigerate shrimp for 30 minutes.

2 Preheat broiler. Broil shrimp about 3 inches from the heat source for 1½ minutes per side or until opaque. Immediately toss hot shrimp with the remaining dressing and red pepper and cool to room temperature. Arrange shrimp on cucumber slices. Makes 20 appetizers.

PER APPETIZER		DAILY GOAL
Calories	25	2,000 (F), 2,500 (M)
Total fat	1 g	60 g or less (F), 70 g or less (M)
Saturated fat	0 g	20 g or less (F), 23 g or less (M)
Cholesterol	28 mg	300 mg or less
Sodium	41 mg	2,400 mg or less
Carbohydrates	1 g	250 g or more
Protein	4 g	55 g to 90 g

CLEANING SHRIMP

There's no question, shrimp is a number one favorite cocktail food! Don't be daunted by the job of cleaning shrimp yourself. It's a snap. With kitchen scissors, cut the shell, following the curve of the outer back, moving from the top toward the tail to expose the dark vein. Rinse under cold water while slipping off the shell and the vein. Drain and pat dry on paper towels.

NOTES

SMOKED SALMON RIBBON SANDWICHES

These elegant sandwiches are perfect with cocktails or as part of an elegant tea service.

Prep time: 1 hour plus chilling
○ *Degree of difficulty: easy*

Smoked Salmon Filling

- 4 ounces cream cheese, softened
- 3 ounces smoked salmon, chopped
- 1 tablespoon heavy *or* whipping cream
- 2 teaspoons fresh lemon juice
- ⅛ teaspoon freshly ground pepper

Watercress Filling

- 1 cup firmly packed watercress leaves
- ⅓ cup mayonnaise *or* salad dressing
- 1 ounce cream cheese, softened

- 15 slices very thinly sliced whole wheat bread
- 10 slices very thinly sliced white bread
- ¼ cup butter, softened (no substitutions)

1 For Smoked Salmon Filling, process the cream cheese, salmon, cream, lemon juice, and pepper in a food processor until smooth. Remove mixture from processor bowl and set aside.

2 For Watercress Filling, process the watercress, mayonnaise, and cream cheese in food processor until well combined.

3 Lightly spread 1 side of all bread slices with butter. Spread 1 generous tablespoon of salmon filling on each of 10 slices of whole wheat bread. Spread 1 tablespoon of watercress filling on each of 10 slices of white bread. Make a stack of 2 alternating layers each of salmon and watercress slices, then top with 1 whole wheat slice, buttered side down. Repeat process, making 5 sandwich stacks.

4 Wrap sandwiches in wax paper and arrange on a cookie sheet. Place a second cookie sheet on top to weight lightly. Refrigerate 1 hour or up to 24 hours. To serve, unwrap sandwiches, trim crusts, and slice into ½-inch-wide strips. Arrange on trays. Makes about 30 sandwich strips.

PER STRIP		DAILY GOAL
Calories	80	2,000 (F), 2,500 (M)
Total fat	6 g	60 g or less (F), 70 g or less (M)
Saturated fat	2 g	20 g or less (F), 23 g or less (M)
Cholesterol	12 mg	300 mg or less
Sodium	123 mg	2,400 mg or less
Carbohydrates	5 g	250 g or more
Protein	2 g	55 g to 90 g

NOTES

_____

_____

_____

_____

_____

_____

_____

_____

_____

_____

_____

_____

_____

93

SHRIMP TOASTS WITH SOY DIPPING SAUCE

We all love these crisp, golden treats in Chinese take-out, but when they're prepared from scratch you won't believe the difference! Cooked up in a flash, they're completely do-ahead for company.

Prep time: 35 minutes
Cooking time: 1 to 1½ minutes per batch
 *Degree of difficulty: moderate*

Toasts

- 1 **pound medium shrimp, peeled and deveined**
- ¼ **cup chopped water chestnuts**
- 1 **large egg white**
- 4 **teaspoons dry sherry**
- 1 **tablespoon minced green onion**
- 1 **tablespoon cornstarch**
- 1 **teaspoon grated fresh ginger**
- ¾ **teaspoon salt**
- ¼ **teaspoon hot chile oil**

12 **slices firm white sandwich bread, crusts trimmed**
   Vegetable oil, for frying

Sauce

- ¼ **cup soy sauce**
- 2 **tablespoons dry sherry**
- 2 **teaspoons minced green onion**
- ½ **teaspoon grated fresh ginger**
- ¼ **teaspoon Asian sesame oil**

1 Coarsely chop the shrimp. Place the water chestnuts, egg white, sherry, green onion, cornstarch, ginger, salt, and chile oil in a food processor. Pulse, turning machine on and off, for 5 to 8 seconds or until mixture is finely chopped.

2 Cut each bread slice diagonally into 4 triangles. Spread triangles evenly on 1 side with a thin layer of shrimp mixture.

3 Heat ½ inch of vegetable oil in a large deep skillet to 375°F. Add triangles, a few at a time, shrimp side down, to hot oil. Fry for 1 to 1½ minutes or until golden, turning once. Drain on paper towels. (Can be made ahead. Cool, then cover and refrigerate overnight. To reheat, place on a cookie sheet and bake in a preheated 350°F. oven 10 minutes until hot.)

4 For sauce, combine the soy sauce, sherry, onion, ginger, and sesame oil in a small bowl. Transfer toasts to a serving platter and serve with sauce. Makes 48 appetizers.

PER APPETIZER		DAILY GOAL
Calories	40	2,000 (F), 2,500 (M)
Total fat	2 g	60 g or less (F), 70 g or less (M)
Saturated fat	0 g	20 g or less (F), 23 g or less (M)
Cholesterol	12 mg	300 mg or less
Sodium	167 mg	2,400 mg or less
Carbohydrates	4 g	250 g or more
Protein	2 g	55 g to 90 g

NOTES

_____

_____

_____

_____

_____

_____

_____

_____

_____

SHRIMP PINWHEEL SANDWICHES

Pretty and pink, the shrimp filling is accented by just a touch of dry sherry.

Prep time: 30 minutes plus chilling
Cooking time: 2 minutes
○ *Degree of difficulty: easy*

½ **pound medium shrimp, peeled and deveined**
¼ **cup mayonnaise**
1 **tablespoon fresh lemon juice**
1 **tablespoon dry sherry**
⅛ **teaspoon salt**
¼ **teaspoon freshly ground pepper**
2 **tablespoons chopped fresh parsley**
14 **slices very thinly sliced white bread**
2 **tablespoons butter, softened (no substitutions)**

1 Heat a medium saucepan of water to boiling. Add the shrimp and cook about 2 minutes or until pink and opaque. Drain well. Place shrimp, mayonnaise, lemon juice, sherry, salt, and pepper in a food processor and process until smooth. Transfer to a small bowl and stir in the parsley.

2 Trim the crusts from the bread. Place 2 slices end to end, overlapping by ½ inch. With a rolling pin, roll bread into a very thin 7x4-inch rectangle. Spread lightly with butter, then spread with 2 tablespoons of the shrimp mixture. Roll bread up tightly from the short side, jelly-roll fashion. Wrap in plastic wrap and refrigerate up to 4 hours. Repeat process with remaining bread.

3 To serve, unwrap the rolls and slice thin. Arrange pinwheels on serving trays. Makes about 6 dozen pinwheels.

PER SANDWICH		DAILY GOAL
Calories	20	2,000 (F), 2,500 (M)
Total fat	1 g	60 g or less (F), 70 g or less (M)
Saturated fat	g	20 g or less (F), 23 g or less (M)
Cholesterol	5 mg	300 mg or less
Sodium	29 mg	2,400 mg or less
Carbohydrates	1 g	250 g or more
Protein	1 g	55 g to 90 g

POTTED SHRIMP

"Potted" describes meat or fish that is ground and packed in a dish. This lovely version using shrimp is perfect served with crackers, cucumber slices, sugar snap peas, or Belgian endive spears.

Prep time: 20 minutes plus cooling
Cooking time: 30 minutes
○ *Degree of difficulty: easy*

- 4 **cups water**
- 1 **cup dry white wine**
- 1 **medium onion, chopped**
- 1 **teaspoon salt**
- 1 **bay leaf**
- ¼ **teaspoon thyme**
- 1½ **pounds medium shrimp, in shells**
- ¾ **cup butter, softened (no substitutions)**
- 3 **tablespoons fresh lemon juice**
- ½ **teaspoon ground red pepper**

1 Combine the water, wine, onion, salt, bay leaf, and thyme in a large saucepan and bring to a boil. Add the shrimp and cook about 3 minutes or just until pink. Remove shrimp, reserving liquid, and cool.

2 Peel the shrimp, reserving shells; devein and rinse. Return the shells to the cooking liquid and boil 30 minutes. Strain, discarding shells, then return liquid to pan and continue to boil until reduced to ¼ cup. Cool.

3 Combine the cooled liquid, shrimp, butter, lemon juice, and red pepper in a food processor and process until smooth. Spoon into a 1-quart bowl. (Can be made ahead. Cover and refrigerate up to 24 hours. Remove from refrigerator 30 minutes before serving.) Makes 3½ cups.

PER TABLESPOON		DAILY GOAL
Calories	35	2,000 (F), 2,500 (M)
Total Fat	3 g	60 g or less (F), 70 g or less (M)
Saturated fat	2 g	20 g or less (F), 23 g or less (M)
Cholesterol	22 mg	300 mg or less
Sodium	79 mg	2,400 mg or less
Carbohydrates	0 g	250 g or more
Protein	2 g	55 g to 90 g

CAVIAR CROWN MOLD

Here's a layered terrine with something for everyone. Gorgeous layers of egg and avocado, topped off with an indulgent flourish of black and red caviar.

Prep time: 1 hour plus chilling
○ *Degree of difficulty: easy*

- 1 **envelope unflavored gelatin**
  Water

Egg Layer
- 8 **large hard-cooked eggs, finely chopped**
- 1 **cup mayonnaise**
- 2 **tablespoons minced fresh parsley**
- ¼ **cup minced green onions**
- 1 **teaspoon salt**
- ⅛ **teaspoon freshly ground pepper**
  Generous dash hot pepper sauce

Avocado Layer
- ¼ **cup fresh lemon juice**
- 2 **medium ripe avocados, diced**
- 2 **medium ripe avocados, puréed**
- ¼ **cup minced shallots**

¼ cup mayonnaise
1 teaspoon salt
⅛ teaspoon freshly ground pepper
   Generous dash hot pepper sauce

Sour Cream Layer
1 cup sour cream
¼ cup minced green onions
1 jar (2 ounces) black lumpfish
   caviar
1 jar (2 ounces) red lumpfish caviar
   Thinly sliced pumpernickel bread,
   cut into triangles

1 Line bottom and sides of an 8x3-inch springform pan with plastic wrap.

2 Bring 1 inch of water to a boil in a small saucepan. Meanwhile, combine the gelatin and ¼ cup cold water in a 1-cup glass measure. Let stand 5 minutes. Remove saucepan from heat and set cup in hot water. Let stand, stirring occasionally, until gelatin is completely dissolved.

3 For egg layer, combine the eggs, mayonnaise, parsley, green onions, salt, pepper, and red pepper sauce in a large bowl and stir until well blended. Stir in 2 tablespoons of the dissolved gelatin.

(Keep remaining gelatin in hot water bath.) Spoon into prepared springform pan, spreading mixture evenly to the edges. Refrigerate while preparing avocado layer.

4 For avocado layer, stir together the remaining dissolved gelatin and the lemon juice. Combine the diced avocados, puréed avocados, shallots, mayonnaise, salt, pepper, and hot pepper sauce in a large bowl, then stir in dissolved gelatin mixture. Carefully spread mixture evenly over egg layer. Cover pan and refrigerate for 8 hours or until fillings are set. (Can be made ahead. Refrigerate up to 3 days.)

5 For sour cream layer, combine the sour cream and onion in a small bowl. Carefully invert springform pan by uncovering pan and placing a serving plate on top of pan and turning over. Remove sides and bottom of springform pan and plastic wrap. Spread the sour cream mixture evenly over the egg layer.

6 Drain the black caviar in a paper towel-lined sieve. Spoon onto center of mold. Repeat draining with the red caviar and spoon around black caviar. Serve with pumpernickel triangles. Makes 24 servings.

PER SERVING		DAILY GOAL
Calories	200	2,000 (F), 2,500 (M)
Total fat	19 g	60 g or less (F), 70 g or less (M)
Saturated fat	4 g	20 g or less (F), 23 g or less (M)
Cholesterol	110 mg	300 mg or less
Sodium	350 mg	2,400 mg or less
Carbohydrates	4 g	250 g or more
Protein	5 g	55 g to 90 g

HOW MUCH TO SERVE

For light cocktail parties of the pre-dinner variety, plan to serve about 8 hors d'oeuvres per person. For cocktail buffets that may become full meals for your guests, you'll need to double the amount. For these occasions it's a good rule of thumb to plan serving something more substantial such as Mexican Meatballs (recipe, page 98) or Swedish Meatballs (recipe, page 100), baked ham with Cornmeal-Buttermilk Biscuits (recipe, page 89), or Spicy Pork Tenderloin with Lime Mayonnaise (recipe, page 101).

MEXICAN MEATBALLS

Zarela Martinez, chef and owner of Zarela's, a Manhattan hot spot, learned to make these memorable meatballs from her mother, Aida.

Prep time: 45 minutes plus chilling
Cooking time: 45 minutes
Degree of difficulty: easy

6 garlic cloves, divided
1½ teaspoons salt, divided
½ cup masa harina*
¼ cup warm water
1 pound lean ground pork
1 pound lean ground beef
1 large egg
½ teaspoon freshly ground pepper
2 cans (28 ounces each) tomatoes, drained
3 canned chipotle chiles in adobo,* drained
¼ cup vegetable oil
½ cup chopped onion
2 tablespoons instant chicken bouillon granules
1 teaspoon cumin
Fresh parsley *or* cilantro, for garnish

1 Mash 4 of the garlic cloves to a paste with ½ teaspoon of the salt in a small bowl. Combine the masa harina with the water in a large bowl. Add the pork, beef, egg, garlic paste, the remaining 1 teaspoon of salt, and pepper and mix well. Shape mixture into 1-inch balls.

2 In a blender, purée the tomatoes with the remaining 2 garlic cloves until smooth, then force mixture through a sieve into a small bowl. Purée the chiles and 1 cup water in the blender and strain into another small bowl.

3 Heat the oil in a large Dutch oven over medium heat. Add the onion and cook, stirring, 2 minutes. Add tomato purée, cover, and cook 5 minutes. Stir in the bouillon granules and cumin and cook 2 minutes. Gradually add chile purée, tasting for spiciness after each addition.

4 Add meatballs and bring to a boil. Cover and cook 3 minutes. Reduce heat and simmer 30 minutes, turning meatballs. Cool. Cover and refrigerate overnight. (Can be made ahead. Cover and refrigerate up to 3 days or freeze up to 1 month.) Reheat over medium heat, stirring gently, about 30 minutes or until hot. Transfer to a serving bowl and garnish with parsley or cilantro. Makes 7 dozen meatballs.

*Masa harina and canned chipotle chiles can be found in Latin American markets.

PER MEATBALL		DAILY GOAL
Calories	45	2,000 (F), 2,500 (M)
Total fat	3 g	60 g or less (F), 70 g or less (M)
Saturated fat	1 g	20 g or less (F), 23 g or less (M)
Cholesterol	11 mg	300 mg or less
Sodium	160 mg	2,400 mg or less
Carbohydrates	2 g	250 g or more
Protein	2 g	55 g to 90 g

NOTES

SWEDISH MEATBALLS

At any cocktail party in the '50s, meatballs were sure to be served. Even though we've updated this popular hors d'oeuvre with lean beef instead of veal and pork, the taste is irresistibly retro.

Prep time: 20 minutes
Cooking time: 1½ hours
O *Degree of difficulty: easy*

- 4 **tablespoons butter** *or* **margarine, divided**
- 1 **cup finely chopped onions**
- 2 **cups cubed fresh bread**
- ½ **cup milk**
- 1½ **pounds 90% lean ground beef**
- 2 **large eggs**
- 1 **teaspoon salt**
- 1 **teaspoon nutmeg**
- 1 **teaspoon fines herbes**
- 1 **teaspoon paprika**
- 1 **teaspoon dry mustard**
- ¼ **teaspoon freshly ground pepper**
- ¼ **teaspoon minced garlic**
- 2 **tablespoons all-purpose flour**
- 1 **teaspoon tomato paste**
- 1 **cup beef broth**
- ¼ **cup water**
- ½ **cup sour cream**
- 2 **tablespoons chopped fresh dill**

1 Preheat oven to 400°F. Spray 2 jelly-roll pans with vegetable cooking spray.

2 Melt 2 tablespoons of the butter in a large skillet over medium heat. Add the onions and cook about 8 minutes or until tender. Transfer to a large bowl and cool.

3 Soak the bread cubes in the milk in a small bowl 1 minute, then squeeze very dry, discarding milk. Add bread to onions with the beef, eggs, salt, nutmeg, fines herbes, paprika, mustard, and pepper; mix well. Shape into forty 1½-inch balls. Arrange on the prepared jelly-roll pans. Bake for 18 to 20 minutes, turning meatballs once and rotating pans halfway through. Remove meatballs from pans and set aside.

4 Pour 2 tablespoons of water into each jelly-roll pan, scraping up browned bits from bottom. Heat the remaining 2 tablespoons of butter in a large skillet over medium heat. Add the garlic and cook 30 seconds. Stir in the flour and tomato paste and cook 1 minute. Whisk in the beef broth, water, and drippings from jelly-roll pans. Bring to a boil. Add meatballs to skillet. (Can be made ahead. Cover and refrigerate up to 24 hours. Reheat in skillet with ¼ cup more water about 20 minutes or until hot.) Reduce heat to low and stir in the sour cream *(do not boil)*. Sprinkle with dill. Makes 40 meatballs.

PER MEATBALL		DAILY GOAL
Calories	60	2,000 (F), 2,500 (M)
Total fat	4 g	60 g or less (F), 70 g or less (M)
Saturated fat	2 g	20 g or less (F), 23 g or less (M)
Cholesterol	26 mg	300 mg or less
Sodium	121 mg	2,400 mg or less
Carbohydrates	2 g	250 g or more
Protein	4 g	55 g to 90 g

NOTES

_____

_____

_____

_____

_____

_____

_____

_____

SPICY PORK TENDERLOIN WITH LIME MAYONNAISE

For easy entertaining on a budget, here's a great alternative to beef tenderloin.

Prep time: 15 minutes plus chilling
Roasting time: 20 to 25 minutes
Degree of difficulty: easy

- 1 tablespoon minced garlic
- 2 teaspoons paprika
- 1 teaspoon salt
- 1 teaspoon oregano
- 1 teaspoon cumin
- ½ teaspoon ground red pepper
- ½ teaspoon freshly ground pepper
- 2 pork tenderloins (1½ pounds total)
- 2 loaves (1 pound each) French bread, thinly sliced

Lime Mayonnaise
- 1 cup mayonnaise
- 2 tablespoons fresh lime juice
- 1 teaspoon grated lime peel
  Lime wedges and cilantro, for garnish

1 Combine the garlic, paprika, salt, oregano, cumin, and red and black peppers in a small bowl. Rub all over the pork, then wrap and refrigerate overnight.

2 Thirty minutes before roasting, remove pork from refrigerator. Preheat oven to 425°F. Unwrap pork, place in a roasting pan and roast 20 to 25 minutes, until a meat thermometer inserted in thickest part of tenderloin reaches 160°F. Cool to room temperature. (Can be made ahead. Wrap and refrigerate up to 3 days. Remove from refrigerator 30 minutes before serving.)

3 For Lime Mayonnaise, combine the mayonnaise, lime juice, and lime peel in a small bowl. (Can be made ahead. Cover and refrigerate up to 3 days.)

4 To serve, cut pork into very thin slices and serve on French bread with Lime Mayonnaise. Garnish with lime wedges and cilantro. Makes about 80 appetizers.

PER APPETIZER WITH ½ TEASPOON MAYONNAISE AND 1 SLICE BREAD		DAILY GOAL
Calories	63	2,000 (F), 2,500 (M)
Total fat	3 g	60 g or less (F), 70 g or less (M)
Saturated fat	0 g	20 g or less (F), 23 g or less (M)
Cholesterol	7 mg	300 mg or less
Sodium	113 mg	2,400 mg or less
Carbohydrates	7 g	250 g or more
Protein	3 g	55 g to 90 g

NOTES

CURRIED STUFFED EGGS

Prep time: 15 minutes
O *Degree of difficulty: easy*

8 large hard-cooked eggs, halved
¼ cup mayonnaise
2 tablespoons sour cream
1 tablespoon chutney
½ teaspoon curry powder
¼ teaspoon salt
¼ teaspoon freshly ground pepper
  Paprika, for garnish

Place the egg yolks, mayonnaise, sour cream, chutney, curry, salt, and pepper in a blender or food processor. Process until mixture is smooth. With a pastry bag or spoon, fill egg white halves. Sprinkle with paprika. Makes 16 half eggs.

PER HALF EGG		DAILY GOAL
Calories	70	2,000 (F), 2,500 (M)
Total fat	6 g	60 g or less (F), 70 g or less (M)
Saturated fat	1 g	20 g or less (F), 23 g or less (M)
Cholesterol	109 mg	300 mg or less
Sodium	87 mg	2,400 mg or less
Carbohydrates	1 g	250 g or more
Protein	3 g	55 g to 90 g

COOL IT

Don't try to keep your party beverages cold in the fridge—when it's party time you'll need the space. Instead look for large tin buckets (they're inexpensive) and fill them with ice and drinks.

NOTES

SAVORY STUFFED MUSHROOMS

A classic vegetarian appetizer, these fragrant morsels use the whole mushroom—stems and all.

▽ *Low-calorie*
   Prep time: 30 minutes
   Cooking time: 30 to 32 minutes
○ *Degree of difficulty: easy*

   2 **pounds medium fresh mushrooms**
   1 **cup fresh bread crumbs**
   3 **tablespoons butter** *or* **margarine**
   ½ **cup minced red pepper**
   ¼ **cup minced shallots**
   ½ **cup shredded mozzarella cheese**
   3 **tablespoons freshly grated Parmesan cheese**
   3 **tablespoons chopped fresh parsley, divided**
   ¼ **teaspoon freshly cracked pepper**
   Salt

1 Preheat oven to 350°F. Grease a jelly roll pan. Remove the stems from the mushroom caps, then chop stems and transfer to a medium bowl.

2 Toast the bread crumbs on a cookie sheet for 7 to 8 minutes until golden.

3 Meanwhile, melt the butter in a medium skillet over medium heat. Add the red pepper and shallots and cook for 3 to 4 minutes or until tender. Add to the bowl with the mushroom stems. Stir in the toasted bread crumbs, mozzarella, Parmesan, 2 tablespoons of the parsley, and the cracked pepper.

4 Lightly salt the inside of the mushroom caps. Spoon stuffing mixture evenly in centers, then arrange mushrooms on prepared pan. Sprinkle remaining 1 tablespoon parsley over tops. (Can be made ahead. Cover and refrigerate up to 4 hours.) Bake about 20 minutes or until filling is hot and mushroom caps are tender. Makes about 3 dozen appetizers.

PER APPETIZER		DAILY GOAL
Calories	30	2,000 (F), 2,500 (M)
Total fat	2 g	60 g or less (F), 70 g or less (M)
Saturated fat	1 g	20 g or less (F), 23 g or less (M)
Cholesterol	4 mg	300 mg or less
Sodium	94 mg	2,400 mg or less
Carbohydrates	2 g	250 g or more
Protein	1 g	55 g to 90 g

NOTES

DEVILS ON HORSEBACK

This hot hors d'oeuvre graced the pages of *Ladies' Home Journal* during the 1920's. A classic combination of sweet and salty, we decided these tasty morsels were ready for a comeback.

Prep time: 20 minutes
Broiling time: 3 to 4 minutes
○ *Degree of difficulty: easy*

2   dozen pitted prunes
¼   cup chopped stuffed green olives
12 slices bacon, halved

Preheat broiler. Cut a slit lengthwise in each prune then spoon ½ teaspoon of chopped olives into each cavity. Wrap prunes in bacon and secure with toothpicks. Arrange on a broiler pan and broil for 3 to 4 minutes or until bacon is crisp. Serve hot. Makes 2 dozen appetizers.

PER APPETIZER		DAILY GOAL
Calories	40	2,000 (F), 2,500 (M)
Total fat	2 g	60 g or less (F), 70 g or less (M)
Saturated fat	1 g	20 g or less (F), 23 g or less (M)
Cholesterol	3 mg	300 mg or less
Sodium	85 mg	2,400 mg or less
Carbohydrates	5 g	250 g or more
Protein	1 g	55 g to 90 g

TIMING IS EVERYTHING

How much time to allot for cocktails and hors d'oeuvres before serving dinner? Dinner should always be planned at least an hour later than the invitation indicates, but cocktails should last no longer than an hour and a half.

HAM MOUSSE IN CUCUMBER CUPS

Good quality baked ham is essential for this appetizer and we love the Black Forest variety for its marvelous smoky flavor.

▽ *Low-calorie*
  Prep time: 25 minutes
○ *Degree of difficulty: easy*

½ **pound Black Forest ham**
1 **package (3 ounces) cream cheese**
¼ **cup toasted ground walnuts**
2 **tablespoons mayonnaise**
1 **tablespoon Dijon mustard**
1 **tablespoon minced shallots**
½ **teaspoon freshly ground pepper**
4 **cucumbers**
  Fresh parsley sprigs and toasted walnuts, for garnish

1 Place the ham in a food processor fitted with a steel blade and pulse the machine until ham is finely chopped. Add the cream cheese, walnuts, mayonnaise, mustard, shallots, and pepper and process until smooth. Spoon mixture into a pastry bag fitted with a star tip.

2 Peel the cucumbers, leaving some strips of skin. Cut into ¾-inch-thick slices. With a melon baller, scoop out the center of each slice. Pipe ham mousse into cucumber cups. Garnish with parsley and walnuts. Makes 3 dozen appetizers.

PER APPETIZER		DAILY GOAL
Calories	35	2,000 (F), 2,500 (M)
Total fat	3 g	60 g or less (F), 70 g or less (M)
Saturated fat	1 g	20 g or less (F), 23 g or less (M)
Cholesterol	7 mg	300 mg or less
Sodium	118 mg	2,400 mg or less
Carbohydrates	1 g	250 g or more
Protein	2 g	55 g to 90 g

NOTES

SNAPPER PATÉ

An unusual mix of spices makes this simple white fish fabulous. Make this a day ahead to let the flavors mellow.

Prep time: 15 minutes plus cooling
Cooking time: 5 minutes
○ *Degree of difficulty: easy*

1	**pound red snapper** *or* **cod fillets, skinned**
1½	**teaspoons salt, divided**
	Water
2	**tablespoons vegetable oil**
2	**teaspoons minced garlic**
½	**cup minced green onions**
1	**jalapeño chile, seeded and minced**
½	**teaspoon cinnamon**
¼	**teaspoon cumin**
¼	**teaspoon cloves**
½	**cup butter, softened (no substitutions)**
1	**tablespoon fresh lime juice**
	Water biscuits *or* **crackers**
	Sliced green onions and cherry tomatoes, for garnish

1 Place the fish in a large skillet with 1 teaspoon of the salt and enough water to cover. Bring to a simmer and cook 2 minutes. Remove from heat and let stand 10 minutes. Remove fish with a slotted spoon and transfer to a plate; drain liquid.

2 Heat the oil in the same skillet over medium high heat. Add the garlic and cook about 30 seconds or until fragrant. Add the green onions, jalapeño, cinnamon, cumin, and cloves and cook, stirring, 2 minutes. Remove from heat and add the fish. Cool.

3 Process the butter in a food processor until smooth. Add fish mixture, lime juice, and the remaining ½ teaspoon salt; process just until combined. Pack into small crocks. (Can be made ahead. Cover and refrigerate up to 2 days. Remove from refrigerator 30 minutes before serving.) Serve with water biscuits or crackers. Garnish with green onions and cherry tomatoes. Makes 2½ cups.

PER TABLESPOON WITH 1 BISCUIT		DAILY GOAL
Calories	50	2,000 (F), 2,500 (M)
Total fat	3 g	60 g or less (F), 70 g or less (M)
Saturated fat	2 g	20 g or less (F), 23 g or less (M)
Cholesterol	10 mg	300 mg or less
Sodium	90 mg	2,400 mg or less
Carbohydrates	2 g	250 g or more
Protein	3 g	55 g to 90 g

NOTES

_____

_____

_____

_____

_____

_____

_____

_____

_____

_____

_____

_____

MUSTARD STUFFED EGGS

Prep time: 15 minutes
○ *Degree of difficulty: easy*

8 large hard-cooked eggs, halved
⅓ cup mayonnaise
2 tablespoons sour cream
1 teaspoon grated onion
¼ teaspoon dry mustard
¼ teaspoon salt
¼ teaspoon celery seed
⅛ teaspoon ground red pepper
Snipped fresh chives *or* parsley
sprigs, for garnish (optional)

Place the egg yolks, mayonnaise, sour cream, onion, mustard, salt, celery seed, and red pepper in a blender or food processor. Process mixture until smooth. With a pastry bag or spoon, fill egg white halves. Garnish with chives or parsley, if desired. Makes 16 half eggs.

PER HALF EGG		DAILY GOAL
Calories	75	2,000 (F), 2,500 (M)
Total fat	6 g	60 g or less (F), 70 g or less (M)
Saturated fat	2 g	20 g or less (F), 23 g or less (M)
Cholesterol	110 mg	300 mg or less
Sodium	92 mg	2,400 mg or less
Carbohydrates	0 g	250 g or more
Protein	3 g	55 g to 90 g

STOCKING THE BAR

For a party with 20 guests that will last 4 hours or more, you'll need 4 bottles each of dry white and red wine; ½ gallon of vodka; 1 bottle each of gin, bourbon, rum, rye, scotch, and dry vermouth; 2 quarts of orange juice; 1 quart each of grapefruit and cranberry juice; 3 bottles each of tonic water, club soda, and cola; 2 bottles of lemon-lime soda; 1 bottle of ginger ale; fruit slices; and 1 pound of ice per person.

NOTES

SALMON PATÉ

Packed into a pretty crock, this fragrant spread is perfect for cocktails or as part of an elegant brunch.

Prep time: 15 minutes plus standing
Cooking time: 5 minutes
O *Degree of difficulty: easy*

- 1   **pound salmon fillet**
- ¼   **cup dry white wine**
   Water
- ½   **cup unsalted butter, softened (no substitutions)**
- ¼   **pound smoked salmon, chopped**
- 2   **tablespoons fresh lemon juice**
- 2   **tablespoons gin or aquavit (optional)**
- ¾   **teaspoon freshly ground pepper**
   Salt (optional)
   Dill sprigs, for garnish

1 Combine the salmon fillet with the wine and enough water just to cover in a small skillet; bring to a boil. Reduce heat and simmer 5 minutes. Remove from heat and let stand 30 minutes. Drain and flake salmon; discard skin and bones.

2 Place the butter in a food processor and process until creamy. Add smoked salmon, lemon juice, gin (if using), and pepper. Pulse to combine. Add the cooked salmon and pulse just until combined. Taste and add salt if needed. Pack into small crocks. Cover and refrigerate up to 2 days. Before serving, garnish with dill sprigs. (Can be made ahead. Cover and freeze up to 2 weeks. Thaw overnight in refrigerator before serving.) Makes 2½ cups.

PER TABLESPOON		DAILY GOAL
Calories	40	2,000 (F), 2,500 (M)
Total fat	3 g	60 g or less (F), 70 g or less (M)
Saturated fat	2 g	20 g or less (F), 23 g or less (M)
Cholesterol	13 mg	300 mg or less
Sodium	28 mg	2,400 mg or less
Carbohydrates	0 g	250 g or more
Protein	3 g	55 g to 90 g

NOTES

CHICKEN LIVER-APPLE MOUSSE

In addition to serving this with the usual crackers and assorted vegetables, try sliced apples, too.

Prep time: 15 minutes plus chilling
Cooking time: 10 to 12 minutes
Degree of difficulty: easy

  4 **tablespoons butter, divided
      (no substitutions)**
  ⅓ **cup chopped shallots**
  4 **juniper berries**
  ½ **teaspoon sage**
  1 **medium green apple, peeled,
      cored, and thinly sliced**
  1 **pound chicken livers, trimmed**
  ¾ **teaspoon salt**
  ¼ **teaspoon freshly ground pepper**
  2 **tablespoons cognac *or* brandy**
  ¼ **cup dry Marsala wine**
  ¼ **cup heavy *or* whipping cream**

1 Melt 2 tablespoons of the butter in a large skillet over medium heat. Add the shallots, juniper berries, and sage. Cook and stir mixture for 2 to 3 minutes or until shallots are softened. Add the sliced apple and cook 5 minutes, stirring occasionally, until tender. Add the chicken livers, salt, and pepper and cook until livers are browned but still pink in center. Add the cognac and ignite, then shake the pan to allow the flame to die out. Stir in the Marsala and cover and simmer for 3 to 4 minutes or until liquid has thickened. Transfer liver mixture to a medium bowl and cool to room temperature.

2 Process liver mixture in a food processor or blender with the remaining 2 tablespoons of butter until smooth. With the machine on, add the cream in a steady stream until mixture is blended. Transfer mousse to a serving dish and cover surface directly with plastic wrap. Refrigerate at least 2 hours or overnight. (Can be made ahead. Cover and refrigerate up to 2 days.) Makes 2 cups.

PER TABLESPOON		DAILY GOAL
Calories	45	2,000 (F), 2,500 (M)
Total fat	3 g	60 g or less (F), 70 g or less (M)
Saturated fat	1 g	20 g or less (F), 23 g or less (M)
Cholesterol	69 mg	300 mg or less
Sodium	78 mg	2,400 mg or less
Carbohydrates	1 g	250 g or more
Protein	3 g	55 g to 90 g

NOTES

PESTO STUFFED EGGS

It doesn't matter how many of these you make—you'll run out. The pesto filling is mildly flavored with basil and pine nuts, and can be made ahead, covered, and refrigerated up to 8 hours.

Prep time: 30 minutes
○ *Degree of difficulty: easy*

   8 **large hard-cooked eggs, halved**
  ⅓ **cup fresh basil leaves**
  ¼ **cup mayonnaise**
   2 **tablespoons butter *or* margarine, softened**
   2 **tablespoons freshly grated Parmesan cheese**
   2 **teaspoons pine nuts (pignoli)**
   1 **small garlic clove, quartered**
   3 **tablespoons warm water**
      Salt (optional)
      Pine nuts (pignoli) and basil leaves, for garnish

Place the egg yolks, basil, mayonnaise, butter, Parmesan, pine nuts, and garlic in a blender or food processor. Process the mixture until smooth. With the machine on, add the warm water. Taste for seasoning, adding salt if needed. With a pastry bag or spoon, fill egg white halves. Garnish with additional pine nuts and basil leaves. Makes 16 half eggs.

PER HALF EGG		DAILY GOAL
Calories	80	2,000 (F), 2,500 (M)
Total fat	7 g	60 g or less (F), 70 g or less (M)
Saturated fat	2 g	20 g or less (F), 23 g or less (M)
Cholesterol	113 mg	300 mg or less
Sodium	79 mg	2,400 mg or less
Carbohydrates	1 g	250 g or more
Protein	3 g	55 g to 90 g

SPINACH CHEESE ROLLS

Here's an appetizer that is totally freezer-friendly for do-ahead ease, and it can easily be doubled for a big crowd.

Prep time: 35 minutes
Baking time: 20 minutes
 Degree of difficulty: moderate

- **8 tablespoons butter, divided (no substitutions)**
- **¼ cup chopped onion**
- **1 bag (10 ounces) fresh spinach, rinsed, drained, and chopped, *or* 1 package (10 ounces) frozen chopped spinach, thawed and squeezed dry**
- **½ cup ricotta cheese *or* small-curd cottage cheese**
- **½ cup (2 ounces) crumbled feta cheese**
- **1 large egg, lightly beaten**
- **⅛ to ¼ teaspoon salt**
- **⅛ teaspoon nutmeg**
- **⅛ teaspoon freshly ground pepper**
- **9 sheets phyllo dough**
- **¼ cup plain dry bread crumbs**

1 For filling, melt 1 tablespoon of the butter in a medium skillet over medium heat. Add the onion and cook about 5 minutes or until softened. Add the spinach and cook, stirring constantly, for 2 to 3 minutes or until moisture is evaporated. Remove from heat and stir in ricotta, feta, egg, salt, nutmeg, and pepper. Set aside.

2 Preheat oven to 375°F. Grease a cookie sheet. Melt the remaining 7 tablespoons of butter in a small skillet. Place 1 phyllo sheet lengthwise on a sheet of wax paper or clean towel. (Keep remaining phyllo covered with a damp towel.) Brush lightly with melted butter and sprinkle with 1 tablespoon bread crumbs. Repeat layering and buttering 2 more phyllo sheets, then spread a third of the filling along 1 long edge of phyllo.

3 Using wax paper as a guide, roll phyllo from long edge jelly-roll fashion. Place phyllo roll seam-side down on prepared cookie sheet and press ends to seal. Brush the top with butter. With a sharp knife, cut slices about halfway through phyllo roll at 1-inch intervals. Repeat process 2 more times with remaining phyllo, butter, bread crumbs, and filling to make 2 more rolls.

(Can be made ahead. Wrap rolls well in plastic wrap and foil and freeze up to 1 month. To bake, brush with 1 additional tablespoon butter, melted.)

4 Bake rolls about 20 minutes or until golden brown. (If frozen, bake an additional 15 to 20 minutes.) While still warm, cut rolls into slices. Makes about 45 appetizers.

PER APPETIZER		DAILY GOAL
Calories	45	2,000 (F), 2,500 (M)
Total fat	3 g	60 g or less (F), 70 g or less (M)
Saturated fat	2 g	20 g or less (F), 23 g or less (M)
Cholesterol	13 mg	300 mg or less
Sodium	77 mg	2,400 mg or less
Carbohydrates	3 g	250 g or more
Protein	1 g	55 g to 90 g

NOTES

_____

_____

_____

_____

_____

_____

_____

MINI PUFFS WITH GOAT CHEESE AND HERBS

These hot appetizers are made with the classic French choux pastry puffs—a rich egg dough stirred up right in a saucepan.

Prep time: 35 minutes
Baking time: 20 to 25 minutes
Degree of difficulty: moderate

Pastry

- ¼ **cup water**
- ¼ **cup milk**
- ¼ **cup butter *or* margarine, cut up**
- **Pinch salt**
- **Pinch nutmeg**
- ⅔ **cup all-purpose flour**
- 3 **large eggs, divided**

Filling

- 1 **package (3 ounces) cream cheese with chives, softened**
- 1 **log (3 ounces) goat cheese, softened**
- 3 **tablespoons milk**
- 1 **tablespoon chopped fresh parsley**
- 2 **teaspoons chopped fresh dill *or* basil**
- ⅛ **teaspoon freshly ground pepper Dill sprigs, for garnish**

1 Preheat oven to 375°F. Grease a cookie sheet. Set aside. For pastry, bring the water, milk, butter, salt, and nutmeg to a boil in a large saucepan, stirring until butter melts. Remove from heat and stir in the flour with a wooden spoon. Add 2 of the eggs, 1 at a time, stirring vigorously with the spoon until a stiff batter is formed. Spoon batter into a pastry bag fitted with a ½-inch plain tip.

2 Pipe twenty-four 1-inch puffs (or spoon batter with a rounded measuring teaspoon) 1 inch apart onto the prepared cookie sheet. Lightly beat the remaining egg and brush over tops of puffs. Bake for 20 to 25 minutes or until golden brown. Transfer to a wire rack and cool. (Can be made ahead. Cover and freeze up to 2 weeks. Thaw at room temperature 30 minutes.) Slice puffs in half horizontally with a serrated knife. Remove any soft dough from centers.

3 For filling, beat the cream cheese, goat cheese, and milk in a medium bowl until smooth. Add the parsley, dill, and pepper and mix well. Pipe filling with a pastry bag, or spread a scant tablespoon mixture, in bottom half of each puff. Replace tops. (Can be made ahead. Cover and freeze in an airtight container up to 2 weeks. Bake in a preheated 375°F. oven 10 minutes.) Garnish with dill, if desired. Makes 2 dozen puffs.

PER PUFF		DAILY GOAL
Calories	65	2,000 (F), 2,500 (M)
Total fat	5 g	60 g or less (F), 70 g or less (M)
Saturated fat	3 g	20 g or less (F), 23 g or less (M)
Cholesterol	39 mg	300 mg or less
Sodium	69 mg	2,400 mg or less
Carbohydrates	3 g	250 g or more
Protein	2 g	55 g to 90 g

NOTES

_____

_____

_____

_____

_____

_____

_____

_____

BAKED BRIE WITH MANGO CHUTNEY AND ALMONDS

We've taken one of our most popular creamy cheeses and made it even more indulgent.

Prep time: 10 minutes
Baking time: 15 minutes
○ *Degree of difficulty: easy*

1 **small wheel (2¼ pounds)**
   Brie cheese
½ **cup mango chutney**
⅓ **cup sliced blanched almonds**
2 **red apples, sliced**
1 **package melba toast**

Preheat oven to 350°F. Place the Brie on a cookie sheet and spread the chutney on top, leaving a ½-inch border. Place the almonds around the border. Bake for 15 minutes. Carefully transfer warm Brie to a large cheese board or cutting board and surround with the apples and melba toast. Makes 16 to 20 servings.

PER SERVING		DAILY GOAL
Calories	254	2,000 (F), 2,500 (M)
Total fat	17 g	60 g or less (F), 70 g or less (M)
Saturated fat	0 g	20 g or less (F), 23 g or less (M)
Cholesterol	57 mg	300 mg or less
Sodium	474 mg	2,400 mg or less
Carbohydrates	12 g	250 g or more
Protein	13 g	55 g to 90 g

NOTES

116

CHEESE AND ARTICHOKE CRESCENTS

Super-flaky puff pastry is the perfect casing for this melt-in-your mouth filling of cheese, chopped artichoke, and a touch of garlic.

Prep time: 40 minutes
Baking time: 15 minutes
Degree of difficulty: moderate

- ¾ **cup chopped frozen artichoke hearts, thawed**
- ⅓ **cup plain dry bread crumbs**
- ¼ **cup freshly grated Parmesan cheese**
- ¼ **cup shredded Jarlsberg *or* Gruyère cheese**
- ¼ **cup chopped fresh parsley**
- 2 **large eggs, divided**
- 1 **teaspoon minced garlic**
- ¼ **teaspoon salt**
- ⅛ **teaspoon freshly ground pepper**
- 2 **packages (17¼ ounces each) frozen puff pastry, thawed**

1 Preheat oven to 425°F. Combine the artichokes, bread crumbs, Parmesan, Jarlsberg, parsley, 1 of the eggs, garlic, salt, and pepper in a small bowl.

2 Between 2 sheets of lightly floured wax paper, roll the puff pastry ⅛-inch thick. Cut with a 3-inch round biscuit cutter into 48 circles. Beat the remaining egg and brush over circles. Refrigerate 10 minutes Spoon 1 rounded teaspoon filling on each circle and fold dough over filling then press edges to seal.

3 Brush tops of crescents with beaten egg and transfer to an ungreased cookie sheet. Bake about 15 minutes or until puffed and browned. Serve hot. (Can be made ahead. Cool crescents on a wire rack then wrap well in plastic wrap and foil and freeze up to 1 month. Reheat in a 400°F. oven about 15 minutes.) Makes 4 dozen crescents.

PER CRESCENT		DAILY GOAL
Calories	125	2,000 (F), 2,500 (M)
Total fat	8 g	60 g or less (F), 70 g or less (M)
Saturated fat	1 g	20 g or less (F), 23 g or less (M)
Cholesterol	9 mg	300 mg or less
Sodium	85 mg	2,400 mg or less
Carbohydrates	10 g	250 g or more
Protein	2 g	55 g to 90 g

NOTES

EASY AND ELEGANT

STARTERS

Here are our best beginnings
with an elegant touch, appetizers
that need a knife and a fork—
all designed to impress.
For stunning starters try Shrimp
and Lobster Salad, Oysters
Rockefeller, or Crab Cakes with
Two Sauces. Or, if you're
looking for a first course with a
rustic touch, begin with Mussels
and Mango, Smoked Salmon
Pizza, or Zucchini Ribbons. Any
of these tasty choices will make
your dinner extra special.

ORIENTAL SHRIMP PLATTER

When it's time to party, everybody loves shrimp and this is one of the easiest ways to serve it. If you pick up cooked shrimp at the supermarket fish counter, then all you need to do is whip up the dipping sauce and let your guests make their own nibbles.

▼ *Low-fat*
   Prep time: 10 minutes plus standing
○ *Degree of difficulty: easy*

   3   **tablespoons reduced-sodium soy sauce**
   1   **tablespoon rice vinegar**
   1   **tablespoon chopped green onion**
   1   **teaspoon granulated sugar**
   ½   **teaspoon Oriental sesame oil**
   ¾   **pound peeled, cooked medium shrimp**
   1   **European cucumber, sliced**
   ¼   **cup pink pickled ginger, drained***

1 For dipping sauce, combine the soy sauce, vinegar, onion, sugar, and oil in a small serving bowl.

2 Arrange the shrimp, cucumber, and pickled ginger around sauce on a large platter. Makes 4 servings.

*Pickled ginger is available in the specialty section of some supermarkets and in Asian markets.

PER SERVING		DAILY GOAL
Calories	130	2,000 (F), 2,500 (M)
Total fat	2 g	60 g or less (F), 70 g or less (M)
Saturated fat	0 g	20 g or less (F), 23 g or less (M)
Cholesterol	166 mg	300 mg or less
Sodium	780 mg	2,400 mg or less
Carbohydrates	10 g	250 g or more
Protein	19 g	55 g to 90 g

NOTES

MUSSELS AND MANGO

Preparing classic French cuisine in Paris and New York has served Allen Susser well since he opened Chef Allen's, in North Miami Beach, Florida in 1986. This mussel dish builds on a traditional seafood preparation with mango and coconut milk.

Prep time: 20 minutes
Cooking time: 12 minutes
○ *Degree of difficulty: easy*

2 tablespoons olive oil
¼ cup minced shallots
1 tablespoon minced garlic
20 large mussels (about 2 pounds), scrubbed
½ cup dry white wine
½ cup fresh corn kernels
½ cup diced red pepper
1 teaspoon cumin
1 teaspoon minced Scotch bonnet chile *or* 1 to 2 tablespoons minced jalapeño chile*
1 mango, peeled and finely diced

½ cup unsweetened coconut milk**
Salt
1 tablespoon chopped fresh chervil *or* parsley

1 Heat the oil in a large saucepan over medium-high heat. Add the shallots and cook about 2 minutes or until tender. Add the garlic and mussels and cook about 30 seconds or until fragrant. Add the wine, then cover and simmer for 2 minutes.

2 Sprinkle in the corn, red pepper, cumin and chile, then cover and simmer for 2 minutes. Add the mango and coconut milk and cook, covered, about 5 minutes or until mussels open. *(Discard any unopened mussels.)* Season with the salt and chervil. Arrange mussels in bowls with broth, mango, and vegetables. Makes 4 servings.

*Wear rubber gloves while handling and chopping these extremely hot chiles.

**Unsweetened coconut milk is available in Asian markets, or it can be ordered from Mo-Hotta Mo-Betta, 800-462-3220.

PER SERVING		DAILY GOAL
Calories	265	2,000 (F), 2,500 (M)
Total fat	10 g	60 g or less (F), 70 g or less (M)
Saturated fat	7 g	20 g or less (F), 23 g or less (M)
Cholesterol	18 mg	300 mg or less
Sodium	201 mg	2,400 mg or less
Carbohydrates	21 g	250 g or more
Protein	10 g	55 g to 90 g

NOTES

OYSTERS ROCKEFELLER

This classic appetizer was created in 1899 by Jules Alciatore of Antoine's, in New Orleans. He used watercress but we love the flavor and texture of fresh spinach. *Also pictured on page 110.*

Prep time: 25 minutes
Cooking time: 11 minutes
Degree of difficulty: easy

- **2   pounds fresh spinach, stems removed**
- **⅓   cup butter, melted and divided (no substitutions)**
- **1   tablespoon fresh lemon juice**
- **1   tablespoon anise-flavored liqueur**
- **¼   teaspoon salt**
- **¼   teaspoon ground red pepper**
- **2   dozen shucked oysters on half shells**
- **⅓   cup plain dry bread crumbs**
- **4   slices bacon, cooked**

1 Preheat oven to 475°F. Wash the spinach thoroughly and drain. Place spinach in a large skillet; cover, and cook over medium heat, stirring occasionally, about 3 minutes or until wilted. Drain in a colander. When cool enough to handle, squeeze dry and chop coarsely. Combine spinach in a medium bowl with 4 tablespoons of the melted butter, lemon juice, liqueur, salt, and red pepper.

2 Place oysters in half shells on 2 jelly-roll pans. Spoon about 1 tablespoon spinach mixture on each oyster. Combine the bread crumbs and the remaining butter in a small bowl. Sprinkle about ½ teaspoon crumb mixture evenly on each oyster. Top each with a little crumbled bacon. Bake for 8 minutes. Makes 6 servings.

PER SERVING		DAILY GOAL
Calories	210	2,000 (F), 2,500 (M)
Total fat	14 g	60 g or less (F), 70 g or less (M)
Saturated fat	7 g	20 g or less (F), 23 g or less (M)
Cholesterol	62 mg	300 mg or less
Sodium	461 mg	2,400 mg or less
Carbohydrates	11 g	250 g or more
Protein	9 g	55 g to 90 g

NOTES

123

SHRIMP AND LOBSTER SALAD

Make all the components for this salad ahead of time, then toss just before serving. The crunch comes from a firm, tart apple—the perfect counterpoint to the rich seafood.

Prep time: 25 minutes
O *Degree of difficulty: easy*

Dressing

- ⅓ cup sour cream
- ¼ cup mayonnaise
- ¼ cup chopped fresh chives
- 3 tablespoons chopped fresh tarragon
- 2 tablespoons fresh lemon juice
- 1 teaspoon Dijon mustard
- 1 teaspoon granulated sugar
- ¼ teaspoon salt
- ⅛ teaspoon freshly ground pepper

Salad

- 1 teaspoon salt
- 1 pound medium shrimp, peeled and deveined
- ½ pound cooked lobster meat, coarsely chopped
- 1 Granny Smith apple, diced (1 cup)
- 2 heads Belgian endive, cut into thin strips
- 3 cups watercress, trimmed
  Tarragon sprigs and apple slices, for garnish (optional)

1 For dressing, whisk the sour cream, mayonnaise, chives, tarragon, lemon juice, mustard, sugar, salt, and pepper together in a medium bowl until well blended. (Can be made ahead. Cover and refrigerate up to 8 hours.)

2 For salad, bring a large saucepan of water to a boil over high heat. Add the salt and shrimp and cook about 2 minutes or until shrimp are pink throughout. Rinse under cold running water and pat dry. (Can be made ahead. Cover and refrigerate up to 24 hours.)

3 Just before serving, stir shrimp, lobster, and apple into dressing until thoroughly coated. Toss the endive with the watercress, then arrange on 8 salad plates. Spoon shrimp mixture on top. Garnish with tarragon and apple slices, if desired. Makes 8 servings.

PER SERVING		DAILY GOAL
Calories	165	2,000 (F), 2,500 (M)
Total fat	9 g	60 g or less (F), 70 g or less (M)
Saturated fat	2 g	20 g or less (F), 23 g or less (M)
Cholesterol	99 mg	300 mg or less
Sodium	380 mg	2,400 mg or less
Carbohydrates	5 g	250 g or more
Protein	16 g	55 g to 90 g

NOTES

SMOKED SALMON PIZZA

This first course pizza is pure indulgence! Don't skimp on the topping ingredients. Using tangy crème fraîche and premium smoked salmon makes all the difference in taste.

Prep time: 15 minutes plus rising
Baking time: 8 to 10 minutes
○ *Degree of difficulty: easy*

Dough

- 3 **cups all-purpose flour**
- 1 **package (¼ ounce) active dry yeast**
- ¾ **to 1 cup hot water (120°F. to 130°F.)**
- 3 **tablespoons olive oil, divided**
- 1 **tablespoon honey**
  Salt
  Freshly ground pepper

Topping

- ½ **cup crème fraîche *or* sour cream**
- 8 **ounces thinly sliced smoked salmon**
- 2 **teaspoons minced chives**
- 4 **lemon wedges**

1 For dough, combine the flour and yeast in a large mixing bowl. Add the water, 2 tablespoons of the olive oil, the honey, and 1 teaspoon salt and beat at high speed until dough forms a ball.

2 Transfer dough to a lightly floured surface and knead about 5 minutes or until smooth and elastic. Place dough in a greased bowl, turning to grease top. Cover with a clean kitchen towel and let rise in a warm, draft-free place for 30 minutes. Divide dough into quarters and roll each piece into a tight ball. Place balls on a lightly greased cookie sheet. Cover with a damp towel and refrigerate at least 1 hour or overnight.

3 Preheat oven to 500°F. Lightly oil 2 cookie sheets. Remove dough from refrigerator and roll each piece of dough into an 8-inch circle. Place 2 circles on each prepared cookie sheet. Brush circles with the remaining tablespoon of olive oil and sprinkle lightly with salt and pepper. Bake 8 to 10 minutes, rotating cookie sheets halfway through baking if necessary, until crusts are golden brown.

4 Place each pizza on a serving plate. Spread 2 tablespoons of crème fraîche over each and cover evenly with the smoked salmon. Sprinkle tops with minced chives and serve each pizza with a wedge of lemon. Makes 4 servings.

PER SERVING		DAILY GOAL
Calories	580	2,000 (F), 2,500 (M)
Total fat	19 g	60 g or less (F), 70 g or less (M)
Saturated fat	6 g	20 g or less (F), 23 g or less (M)
Cholesterol	26 mg	300 mg or less
Sodium	1,013 mg	2,400 mg or less
Carbohydrates	79 g	250 g or more
Protein	22 g	55 g to 90 g

NOTES

GRAVLAX

This must be prepared at least two days in advance. The salmon "cooks" in the refrigerator with the help of a curing rub made of salt, sugar, dill, and gin.

Prep time: 20 minutes plus marinating
Degree of difficulty: easy

2 **same-size pieces salmon fillets with skin (about 2½ pounds)**
¼ **cup salt**
¼ **cup granulated sugar**
2 **tablespoons ground white pepper**
1 **tablespoon crushed juniper berries**
1 **large bunch fresh dill, trimmed**
3 **tablespoons gin**

Mustard-Dill Sauce
1½ **teaspoons dry mustard**
1 **tablespoon gin**
1 **cup mayonnaise**
¼ **cup chopped fresh dill**
2 **tablespoons Dijon mustard**
1 **tablespoon fresh lemon juice**
  Small dill sprigs, for garnish (optional)
  Toast triangles

1 Rinse the salmon under cold running water and pat dry. Stir together the salt, sugar, pepper, and juniper berries. Rub a generous amount of the mixture into the skin of 1 piece of salmon. Place skin side down in a shallow glass or ceramic dish. Sprinkle with some more of the salt mixture, then top with dill and sprinkle with gin. Top with the second piece of salmon, skin side up. Rub skin with remaining salt mixture. Cover with plastic wrap. Weight down with a cutting board that fits just inside the dish, topped with several heavy cans. Cover and refrigerate 48 hours or up to 1 week, turning every 12 hours and spooning juice over fish.

2 For Mustard-Dill Sauce, dissolve the dry mustard in the gin in a small bowl. Let stand 30 minutes. Stir in the mayonnaise, chopped dill, and mustard. (Can be made ahead. Cover and refrigerate up to 24 hours.)

3 To serve, remove salmon from marinade. Scrape away dill and spices and pat dry. Place salmon skin side down on a cutting board, then cut diagonally into thin slices and remove from skin. Arrange slices on a platter and garnish with dill, if desired. Serve with Mustard-Dill sauce and toast triangles. Makes 12 servings.

PER SERVING		DAILY GOAL
Calories	280	2,000 (F), 2,500 (M)
Total fat	21 g	60 g or less (F), 70 g or less (M)
Saturated fat	3 g	20 g or less (F), 23 g or less (M)
Cholesterol	63 mg	300 mg or less
Sodium	733 mg	2,400 mg or less
Carbohydrates	2 g	250 g or more
Protein	19 g	55 g to 90 g

NOTES

_____

_____

_____

_____

_____

_____

_____

_____

_____

_____

_____

SMOKED TROUT SALAD

By preparing the greens and making the dressing a day ahead, you can have this fancy salad at the table in minutes.

Prep time: 20 minutes

O *Degree of difficulty: easy*

5 tablespoons olive oil
3 tablespoons fresh lemon juice
2 teaspoons prepared horseradish
1 teaspoon Dijon mustard
½ teaspoon salt
½ teaspoon freshly ground pepper
¼ teaspoon granulated sugar
1 head Boston lettuce, separated into leaves
½ head chicory, separated into leaves
1 bunch watercress, trimmed
10 ounces boneless, skinless smoked trout (from about 2 trouts, 8 ounces each), cut into pieces
2 tablespoons minced chives

1 For dressing, whisk the oil, lemon juice, horseradish, mustard, salt, pepper, and sugar together in a small bowl.

2 Arrange the Boston lettuce, chicory, and watercress on a large platter and place fish on top. Sprinkle with chives and drizzle with dressing. Makes 8 servings.

PER SERVING		DAILY GOAL
Calories	130	2,000 (F), 2,500 (M)
Total Fat	9 g	60 g or less (F), 70 g or less (M)
Saturated fat	1 g	20 g or less (F), 23 g or less (M)
Cholesterol	27 mg	300 mg or less
Sodium	441 mg	2,400 mg or less
Carbohydrates	3 g	250 g or more
Protein	10 g	55 g to 90 g

NOTES

TEX-MEX GRILLED SCAMPI

Everyone loves shrimp, and here they're positively sweet and succulent with our zesty sauce spiked with chiles and tequila.

▼ *Low-fat*
▽ *Low-calorie*
   Prep time: 15 minutes plus marinating
   Grilling time: 6 minutes
○ *Degree of difficulty: easy*

Shrimp
- 2 **tablespoons fresh lime juice**
- 2 **tablespoons tequila**
- 1 **tablespoon vegetable oil**
- 2 **jalapeño *or* serrano chiles, thinly sliced**
- ½ **teaspoon salt**
- 1 **pound medium shrimp in shells**

Sauce
- ½ **cup bottled chili sauce**
- 2 **tablespoons minced jalapeño *or* serrano chiles**
- 1 **tablespoon prepared horseradish**
- 1 **tablespoon fresh lime juice**
- 1 **tablespoon tequila**

1 For shrimp, combine the lime juice, tequila, oil, chiles, salt, and shrimp in a medium bowl and toss to blend. Cover and refrigerate 30 minutes or up to 1 hour.

2 Meanwhile, for sauce, combine the chili sauce, jalapeño, horseradish, lime juice, and tequila in a small bowl. Cover and refrigerate until ready to serve.

3 Prepare grill or preheat broiler. Thread shrimp on 6 metal skewers. Grill over medium-hot coals, 4 inches from the heat source, for 2 to 3 minutes per side or until opaque. Serve immediately with sauce. Makes 4 servings.

PER SERVING		DAILY GOAL
Calories	170	2,000 (F), 2,500 (M)
Total fat	3 g	60 g or less (F), 70 g or less (M)
Saturated fat	1 g	20 g or less (F), 23 g or less (M)
Cholesterol	140 mg	300 mg or less
Sodium	732 mg	2,400 mg or less
Carbohydrates	11 g	250 g or more
Protein	20 g	55 g to 90 g

129

FRESH SPRING ROLLS

Similar to egg rolls but never fried, these tasty morsels of Vietnamese origin make refreshing appetizers. A transparent rice wrapper holds the vegetables, herbs, and shrimp in place.

▼ *Low-fat*
▽ *Low-calorie*
   Prep time: 1 hour
○ *Degree of difficulty: easy*

   2 **ounces rice vermicelli noodles***
   2 **cups bean sprouts**
   1 **cup shredded carrots**
   ½ **cup fresh cilantro leaves**
   ½ **cup fresh mint leaves**
  24 **round rice-paper wrappers**
       (8½-inch diameter)*
   8 **leaves Boston lettuce, torn in**
       thirds
   2 **dozen medium shrimp, cooked,**
       peeled, deveined, and halved
       lengthwise

Dipping Sauce
   ½ **cup water**
   2 **tablespoons granulated sugar**
   2 **tablespoons rice wine vinegar**
   1 **tablespoon nuoc mam (fish sauce)***
   1 **tablespoon finely shredded carrot**

1 Heat a large saucepan of water to boiling. Add the vermicelli and cook for 1 to 2 minutes or just until tender. Rinse under cold water and drain well.

2 Toss vermicelli with the bean sprouts, carrots, cilantro, and mint leaves until combined. Dip 1 rice-paper wrapper in a bowl of hot water for 10 to 20 seconds or just until softened. (Keep remaining wrappers covered.) Shake off excess water and place on a clean kitchen towel. Place a piece of lettuce on center of wrapper and top with ¼ cup vermicelli mixture. Fold bottom third of wrapper tightly over filling, then fold sides to form an envelope. Place 2 shrimp halves, pink side down, on flap of envelope and roll up tightly. Transfer to a serving plate and cover with a clean, damp towel. Repeat with remaining wrappers, lettuce, vermicelli mixture, and shrimp. (Can be made ahead. Cover with a damp towel and refrigerate up to 6 hours.)

3 For dipping sauce, combine the water and sugar in a small saucepan and bring to a boil, stirring, until sugar is dissolved. Remove from heat and stir in the vinegar, nuoc mam, and carrot. Serve with spring rolls. Makes 2 dozen rolls.

*These items are available in some supermarkets and in Asian markets, or by mail order from Dewildt Imports, 30 Compton Way, Hamilton Square, NJ 08690, 800-338-3433.

PER 2 ROLLS WITH 1 TABLESPOON SAUCE		DAILY GOAL
Calories	60	2,000 (F), 2,500 (M)
Total fat	1 g	60 g or less (F), 70 g or less (M)
Saturated fat	0 g	20 g or less (F), 23 g or less (M)
Cholesterol	31 mg	300 mg or less
Sodium	36 mg	2,400 mg or less
Carbohydrates	7 g	250 g or more
Protein	5 g	55 g to 90 g

NOTES

_____

_____

_____

_____

_____

_____

CRAB CAKES WITH TWO SAUCES

A stand-out appetizer from New York City's famous Rainbow Room, these fabulous crab cakes are made extra special by the addition of 2 tangy sauces

Prep time: 50 minutes plus chilling
Cooking time: 15 minutes
O *Degree of difficulty: easy*

1 **cup mayonnaise**
2 **large egg yolks**
2 **tablespoons dry mustard**
2 **tablespoons chopped fresh tarragon *or* 1 teaspoon dried**
2 **teaspoons Worcestershire sauce**
1 **teaspoon crab boil (Old Bay) seasoning**
¼ **teaspoon red pepper sauce**
¼ **teaspoon salt**
¼ **teaspoon freshly ground pepper**
2 **pounds lump crabmeat, picked over**
2½ **cups fresh bread crumbs**
2 **cups vegetable oil**
  Celery Rémoulade and Creole Mustard Sauce (recipes follow)

1 Combine the mayonnaise, egg yolks, mustard, tarragon, Worcestershire sauce, crab boil seasoning, red pepper sauce, salt, and pepper in a large bowl. Carefully fold in the crab meat.

2 Spread bread crumbs on 2 cookie sheets. Drop crab mixture by tablespoonfuls on top of crumbs. Shape into small cakes; roll in crumbs to coat evenly. Chill 1 hour.

3 Heat oil in a 12-inch skillet over medium heat. Cook cakes in 3 batches about 2 to 3 minutes per side, then transfer to paper towels to drain. (Can be made ahead. Cool. Cover and refrigerate up to 24 hours. Reheat on cookie sheets in a 375°F. oven 15 minutes.) Arrange crab cakes on a warm serving platter. Serve with sauces. Makes about 4 dozen appetizers.

PER APPETIZER		DAILY GOAL
Calories	85	2,000 (F), 2,500 (M)
Total fat	7 g	60 g or less (F), 70 g or less (M)
Saturated fat	1 g	20 g or less (F), 23 g or less (M)
Cholesterol	31 mg	300 mg or less
Sodium	120 mg	2,400 mg or less
Carbohydrates	1 g	250 g or more
Protein	4 g	55 g to 90 g

Celery Rémoulade: Combine ½ cup mayonnaise, ¼ cup chopped chives, 2 tablespoons Dijon mustard, 2 tablespoons fresh lemon juice, and a pinch each of salt and freshly ground pepper in a medium bowl. Add 4 cups julienned celeriac (celery root) or celery and stir until coated. (Can be made ahead. Cover and refrigerate up to 24 hours.) Makes about 4 cups.

PER TABLESPOON		DAILY GOAL
Calories	15	2,000 (F), 2,500 (M)
Total fat	1 g	60 g or less (F), 70 g or less (M)
Saturated fat	0 g	20 g or less (F), 23 g or less (M)
Cholesterol	1 mg	300 mg or less
Sodium	33 mg	2,400 mg or less
Carbohydrates	1 g	250 g or more
Protein	0 g	55 g to 90 g

Creole Mustard Sauce: Combine 1 cup mayonnaise, 1 seeded and minced jalapeño chile or 5 drops red pepper sauce, ½ finely diced sweet red bell pepper, 3 tablespoons Dijon mustard, and 2 tablespoons chopped chives in a medium bowl. (Can be made ahead. Cover and refrigerate up to 24 hours.) Makes 1½ cups.

PER TABLESPOON		DAILY GOAL
Calories	70	2,000 (F), 2,500 (M)
Total fat	7 g	60 g or less (F), 70 g or less (M)
Saturated fat	1 g	20 g or less (F), 23 g or less (M)
Cholesterol	5 mg	300 mg or less
Sodium	97 mg	2,400 mg or less
Carbohydrates	1 g	250 g or more
Protein	0 g	55 g to 90 g

HERBED CLAMS IN WHITE WINE

This spicy Italian broth is great for cooking mussels in, too.

Prep time: 10 minutes
Cooking time: 10 minutes
O *Degree of difficulty: easy*

2 **tablespoons olive oil**
1 **tablespoon minced garlic**
4 **plum tomatoes, seeded and finely chopped**
½ **cup dry white wine**
½ **cup water**
2 **tablespoons fresh lemon juice**
2 **tablespoons chopped fresh oregano**
½ **teaspoon red pepper flakes**
½ **teaspoon freshly ground pepper**
4 **dozen little neck clams *or* quahogs, scrubbed**
   Crusty bread

Heat the oil in a pot over medium-high heat. Add the garlic and tomatoes and cook for 5 minutes. Carefully add the wine, water, lemon juice, oregano, pepper flakes, and pepper. Bring mixture to a simmer. Add the clams, then cover and cook for 5 to 15 minutes or until shells open. *(Discard any unopened clams.)* Arrange clams in bowls with broth and serve immediately with crusty bread. Makes 12 servings.

PER SERVING		DAILY GOAL
Calories	60	2,000 (F), 2,500 (M)
Total fat	3 g	60 g or less (F), 70 g or less (M)
Saturated fat	0 g	20 g or less (F), 23 g or less (M)
Cholesterol	12 mg	300 mg or less
Sodium	22 mg	2,400 mg or less
Carbohydrates	2 g	250 g or more
Protein	5 g	55 g to 90 g

NOTES

MASCARPONE-STUFFED FIGS

Here's a no-cook appetizer that celebrates the tastes of autumn. You can substitute 6 ripe pears, cut into eighths, for the fresh figs if they're hard to find.

▼ *Low-fat*
▽ *Low-calorie*
  Prep time: 25 minutes
○ *Degree of difficulty: easy*

> 6 **ounces thinly sliced prosciutto**
> 12 **fresh figs, quartered**
> ¼ **cup mascarpone cheese** *or* **whipped cream cheese**
> 1 **large fresh lime, quartered**
>   **Freshly ground pepper**

1 Cut each slice of prosciutto lengthwise in half, then crosswise in half again.

2 Top each fig quarter with ¼ teaspoon mascarpone, then wrap in a prosciutto strip. Arrange the wrapped figs on a serving platter. Squeeze a few drops of lime juice over each fig and sprinkle with pepper. Makes 48 appetizers.

PER APPETIZER		DAILY GOAL
Calories	20	2,000 (F), 2,500 (M)
Total fat	1 g	60 g or less (F), 70 g or less (M)
Saturated fat	0 g	20 g or less (F), 23 g or less (M)
Cholesterol	4 mg	300 mg or less
Sodium	66 mg	2,400 mg or less
Carbohydrates	3 g	250 g or more
Protein	1 g	55 g to 90 g

ROASTED POTATOES WITH SOUR CREAM AND CAVIAR

This is an easy last-minute appetizer, perfect to serve when you want to add a fancy first course to any company menu.

  Prep time: 5 minutes
  Roasting time: 25 minutes
○ *Degree of difficulty: easy*

> 2 **tablespoons butter** *or* **margarine, melted**
> 1 **pound small new potatoes**
> ¼ **teaspoon salt**
> ¼ **teaspoon freshly ground pepper**
> ¼ **cup sour cream**
> 2 **tablespoons lumpfish** *or* **salmon caviar**

1 Preheat oven to 400°F. Brush a jelly-roll pan lightly with some of the butter. Slice the potatoes ½-inch thick, discarding ends. Arrange the potato slices on the prepared pan. Brush with the remaining butter and sprinkle with salt and pepper. Bake for 15 minutes. Turn potatoes and bake about 10 minutes more or until tender and golden.

2 Transfer potatoes to a serving platter and keep warm. To serve, spread ½ teaspoon sour cream on each slice and top with ¼ teaspoon lumpfish. Makes about 2 dozen appetizers.

PER APPETIZER		DAILY GOAL
Calories	30	2,000 (F), 2,500 (M)
Total fat	2 g	60 g or less (F), 70 g or less (M)
Saturated fat	1 g	20 g or less (F), 23 g or less (M)
Cholesterol	11 mg	300 mg or less
Sodium	55 mg	2,400 mg or less
Carbohydrates	4 g	250 g or more
Protein	1 g	55 g to 90 g

NOTES

_____

_____

_____

_____

_____

CHICKEN SATE WITH MINT VINAIGRETTE

Here's a favorite appetizer from Wolfgang Puck's world famous Spago restaurant in Los Angeles. Curry-flavored chicken is thinly sliced and grilled. The emerald green sauce complements the flavors beautifully.

Prep time: 40 minutes plus chilling
Grilling time: 3 to 4 minutes
O *Degree of difficulty: easy*

Sate
- 10 **ounces boneless, skinless chicken breast**
- 1 **tablespoon vegetable oil**
- 1½ **teaspoons curry powder**
- 1 **teaspoon freshly ground pepper**
- ½ **teaspoon cumin**
- ¼ **teaspoon salt**

Vinaigrette
- 2 **hard-cooked large egg yolks**
- ¼ **cup rice wine vinegar**
- 2 **tablespoons plus 2 teaspoons finely chopped fresh mint**
- 1 **tablespoon soy sauce**
- ½ **teaspoon coriander**
- ¼ **teaspoon salt**
- ¼ **teaspoon freshly ground pepper**
- ½ **cup vegetable oil**

1 Soak twenty-four 6-inch bamboo skewers in water for 1 hour.

2 For sate, cut the chicken into 24 very thin 3-inch strips. Toss chicken with the oil in a medium bowl. In a small bowl, combine the curry powder, pepper, cumin, and salt. Sprinkle over chicken and toss to coat. Thread 1 chicken strip on each skewer, then cover and refrigerate 1 hour.

3 Meanwhile, for vinaigrette, place the egg yolks, vinegar, 2 tablespoons of the mint, soy sauce, coriander, salt, and pepper in a blender. Blend mixture until smooth. With the machine on, gradually add the oil in a thin, steady stream through the hole in the lid. Transfer the mixture to a small bowl and stir in the remaining 2 teaspoons mint.

4 Prepare grill or preheat broiler. Arrange skewers on a grill or broiler pan as close to the heat source as possible. (Make sure the bare ends of skewers are not directly over or under the flame.) Grill or broil 1½ to

2 minutes per side or until golden. Arrange skewers of chicken on a serving platter around a bowl filled with vinaigrette. Makes 2 dozen appetizers.

PER APPETIZER		DAILY GOAL
Calories	40	2,000 (F), 2,500 (M)
Total fat	3 g	60 g or less (F), 70 g or less (M)
Saturated fat	0 g	20 g or less (F), 23 g or less (M)
Cholesterol	16 mg	300 mg or less
Sodium	64 mg	2,400 mg or less
Carbohydrates	0 g	250 g or more
Protein	3 g	55 g to 90 g

NOTES

_____

_____

_____

_____

_____

_____

_____

_____

_____

_____

THAI DUMPLINGS

These savory dumplings are served with an unusual sweet and sour dipping sauce.

▼ *Low-fat*
Prep time: 1 hour
Cooking time: 15 minutes per batch
◑ *Degree of difficulty: moderate*

Filling

½ **pound shrimp, peeled and deveined**
½ **pound ground pork**
¼ **cup minced green onions**
2 **tablespoons chopped fresh cilantro**
1 **tablespoon minced jalapeño chile**
1 **teaspoon minced garlic**
1 **teaspoon salt**
½ **teaspoon freshly ground pepper**
1 **large egg white**
20 **egg roll wrappers***
40 **fresh cilantro leaves**

Dipping Sauce

½ **cup granulated sugar**
½ **cup distilled vinegar**
1 **cup water**
¼ **cup golden raisins**

1 **tablespoon minced garlic**
1½ **teaspoons fresh ginger**
1 **teaspoon ground red pepper**
½ **teaspoon salt**

1 For filling, chop the shrimp fine. Combine the shrimp, pork, onions, cilantro, jalapeño, garlic, salt, pepper, and egg white in a medium bowl until blended.

2 With a 3-inch round biscuit cutter, cut 40 circles from the egg roll wrappers. Keep wrappers and circles covered with plastic wrap. Place a heaping teaspoon of filling in the center of each circle, then top with a cilantro leaf. Push sides of wrapper up around filling, pinching all around the top to make a frill (some filling should show). Place dumplings on squares of wax paper. Put the wax paper in the water and steam in batches for 15 minutes.

3 For dipping sauce, combine the sugar, vinegar, water, raisins, garlic, ginger, red pepper, and salt in a medium saucepan. Bring to a boil. Reduce heat and simmer 20 minutes. Transfer to a blender and blend until smooth. Serve Dipping Sauce with warm dumplings. Makes 40 dumplings.

*Egg roll wrappers are available in the specialty section of some supermarkets and in Asian markets.

PER DUMPLING WITH 1 TEASPOON SAUCE		DAILY GOAL
Calories	70	2,000 (F), 2,500 (M)
Total fat	2 g	60 g or less (F), 70 g or less (M)
Saturated fat	5 g	20 g or less (F), 23 g or less (M)
Cholesterol	12 mg	300 mg or less
Sodium	163 mg	2,400 mg or less
Carbohydrates	11 g	250 g or more
Protein	3 g	55 g to 90 g

NOTES

_____

_____

_____

_____

_____

_____

_____

_____

_____

_____

POTATO LATKES

Traditionally served at Hanukkah, these delicate potato pancakes are topped with applesauce and sour cream. For a dressier version at party time, try serving these golden fritters with sour cream, snipped chives, smoked salmon, or caviar.

Prep time: 20 minutes
Cooking time: 5 minutes per batch
Degree of difficulty: easy

2   **pounds all-purpose potatoes, peeled**
1   **medium onion**
½   **cup boiling water**
3   **large eggs**
⅓   **cup all-purpose flour**
1   **teaspoon salt**
½   **teaspoon baking powder**
¼   **teaspoon freshly ground pepper**
    Vegetable oil, for frying
    Applesauce and sour cream

1 In a food processor with a shredding blade, process the potatoes. Remove 2 cups potatoes from work bowl and set aside. Shred the onion in the food processor. Replace shredding blade with a metal blade, and coarsely chop potatoes and onions, processing 20 seconds more.

2 Strain off liquid from work bowl, then spoon potato-onion mixture into a large bowl. Pour the boiling water over mixture and mix well. Beat in the eggs, flour, salt, baking powder, and pepper. Stir in reserved shredded potatoes.

3 Preheat oven to 200°F. Meanwhile, heat ½ inch of the oil in a large skillet over medium-high heat. Drop potato batter by the tablespoonful into hot oil, 4 or 5 at a time. Fry until 1 side is golden brown, then turn and brown on the other side, about 5 minutes total. Remove latkes with a slotted spoon and drain on paper towels. Transfer latkes to a cookie sheet and keep warm in preheated oven while cooking remaining potato batter. (Can be made ahead. Cool to room temperature, then cover and refrigerate up to 2 days. Place in a preheated 400°F. oven for 5 to 10 minutes.) Serve with applesauce and sour cream. Makes 25 pancakes.

PER PANCAKE		DAILY GOAL
Calories	55	2,000 (F), 2,500 (M)
Total fat	2 g	60 g or less (F), 70 g or less (M)
Saturated fat	0 g	20 g or less (F), 23 g or less (M)
Cholesterol	25 mg	300 mg or less
Sodium	107 mg	2,400 mg or less
Carbohydrates	7 g	250 g or more
Protein	2 g	55 g to 90 g

FLOWER ICE BUCKET

Next time you serve wine or champagne to guests, try this beautiful serving suggestion.

Fill a metal bowl or ice bucket up two-thirds with water. Place a plastic container about 5 inches in diameter and at least 7 inches high in the water. Weight the container with enough dried beans to submerge it about 6 inches. Center the plastic container and tape rims to secure in position. Cut 3 dozen flowers close to the bud and place in the water. Freeze overnight. Remove the tape and beans and place a hot towel in the plastic container 1 minute. Remove the container. Briefly immerse the bowl or bucket in a pan or sink of hot water and unmold.

ZUCCHINI RIBBONS

Sally Darr, chef and owner of the former La Tulipe restaurant in New York City, transforms ordinary zucchini into an elegant first course. *Also pictured on the cover.*

Prep time: 20 minutes plus standing
Cooking time: 2 to 3 minutes per batch
● *Degree of difficulty: moderate*

Beer Batter
- ¾ **cup sifted all-purpose flour**
- 1 **teaspoon salt**
- 1 **cup beer**

Zucchini Ribbons
- 5 **small zucchini (about 2¼ pounds)**
- 1½ **cups vegetable oil, for frying**
- ¾ **cup all-purpose flour**
- ¼ **teaspoon salt**
- ¼ **teaspoon freshly ground pepper**
- 2 **bunches parsley sprigs, for garnish (optional)**

1 For Beer Batter, place the flour, salt, and beer in a blender container. Blend for 1 minute or until smooth, stopping once to scrape down sides. Transfer batter to a large bowl and let stand at room temperature 3 hours.

2 For Zucchini Ribbons, trim the ends of the zucchini and cut into 4x½-inch strips. In a deep-fat fryer or Dutch oven heat 1 inch oil to 385°F. on a deep-fat thermometer. Combine the flour, salt, and pepper in a large bowl. Dredge about 6 strips zucchini in flour mixture, shaking in a colander to remove excess.

3 Stir the batter, then add zucchini a few strips at a time to coat. Carefully lower the strips into hot oil with a slotted spoon. Fry strips for 2 to 3 minutes or until deep golden brown. Remove with a slotted spoon and drain on paper towels. Repeat process with remaining zucchini, seasoned flour, and batter.

4 Arrange fried zucchini strips, standing upright, in 6 small baskets or on serving plates. Garnish with parsley, if desired. Serve immediately. Makes 6 servings.

PER SERVING		DAILY GOAL
Calories	280	2,000 (F), 2,500 (M)
Total fat	14 g	60 g or less (F), 70 g or less (M)
Saturated fat	2 g	20 g or less (F), 23 g or less (M)
Cholesterol	0 mg	300 mg or less
Sodium	472 mg	2,400 mg or less
Carbohydrates	32 g	250 g or more
Protein	6 g	55 g to 90 g

NOTES

A-C

Artichoke Crescents, Cheese and, 117
Artichokes with Mint, Braised, 47
Asparagus with Tarragon Dipping Sauce, 8
Baba Ghanoush, 24
Bacon and Horseradish Dip, Zesty, 71
Bagna Cauda, 44
Baked Brie with Mango Chutney and Almonds, 116
Baked Ricotta, 40
Beans
 Black Bean Salsa, 58
 Hummus, 24
 No-Guilt Nachos, 69
 Southwest Taco Dip, 60
 Tuscan Beans, 54
Beef
 Korean Barbecued Meatballs, 70
 Mexican Meatballs, 98
 Southwest Taco Dip, 60
 Swedish Meatballs, 100
Black Bean Salsa, 58
Braised Artichokes with Mint, 47
Bread
 Cornmeal-Buttermilk Biscuits, 89
 Focaccia, 38
 Mushroom Tartlets, 86
 Pissaladiére, 37
 Roasted Red Pepper Baguette, 39
 Tomato Bruschetta, 43
Buffalo Chicken Wings, 72
Caponata, 51
Cashews, Sweet and Sassy, 80
Celery Rémoulade, 132
Cheese
 Assorted Crostini, 34
 Baked Brie with Mango Chutney and Almonds, 116
 Baked Ricotta, 40
 Cheese and Artichoke Crescents, 117
 Cheese Crostini, 34
 Cheese Wafers, 74
 Chile Con Queso Dip, 28
 Fried Mozzarella with Anchovy Dip, 77
 Creamy Blue Cheese Dip, 12
 Grilled Quesadilla, 62
 Herbed Yogurt Cheese Dip, 13
 Mascarpone-Stuffed Figs, 135

Cheese *(continued)*
 Microwave Cheese-Chorizo Dip, 65
 Mini Puffs with Goat Cheese and Herbs, 115
 Pepper Jack Empanadas, 66
 Quiche Lorraine Squares, 85
 Roquefort-Walnut Dip, 16
 Spinach Cheese Rolls, 114
 Yankee Grilled Quesadillas, 64
Chicken
 Buffalo Chicken Wings, 72
 Chicken Liver-Apple Mousse, 111
 Chicken Liver Crostini, 35
 Chicken Sate with Mint Vinaigrette, 137
Chile Con Queso Dip, 28
Classic Onion Rings, 76
Classic Salsa Cruda, 29
Cornmeal-Buttermilk Biscuits, 89
Crab Cakes with Two Sauces, 132
Creamy Blue Cheese Dip, 12
Creole Mustard Sauce, 132
Crunchy Jicama Salsa, 21
Curried Stuffed Eggs, 103

D-L

Devils on Horseback, 105
Dip
 Asparagus with Tarragon Dipping Sauce, 8
 Baba Ghanoush, 24
 Bagna Cauda, 44
 Black Bean Salsa, 58
 Chile Con Queso Dip, 28
 Classic Salsa Cruda, 29
 Creamy Blue Cheese Dip, 12
 Crunchy Jicama Salsa, 21
 Double Tomato Jam, 14
 Fresh Spinach Dip, 9
 Fried Mozzarella with Anchovy Dip, 77
 Garden Party Dip, 10
 Grilled Corn and Chile Salsa, 59
 Grilled Eggplant Dip, 17
 Guacamole with a Kick, 26
 Herbed Yogurt Cheese Dip, 13
 Hummus, 24
 Jicama with Chili Dip, 67
 Light Guacamole, 61
 Microwave Cheese-Chorizo Dip, 65
 Roquefort-Walnut Dip, 16
 Salsa Verde, 30

Dip *(continued)*
 Sesame-White Bean Dip, 25
 Skordalia, 19
 Southwest Taco Dip, 60
 Taramasalata, 18
 Zesty Bacon and Horseradish Dip, 71
Double Tomato Jam, 14
Eggplant
 Baba Ghanoush, 24
 Caponata, 51
 Grilled Eggplant Dip, 17
Eggs
 Curried Stuffed Eggs, 103
 Mustard Stuffed Eggs, 108
 Pesto Stuffed Eggs, 112
Empanadas, Pepper Jack, 66
Figs, Mascarpone-Stuffed, 135
Focaccia, 38
Fried Calamari with Creamy Salsa, 79
Fried Mozzarella with Anchovy Dip, 77
Garden Party Dip, 10
Garlic
 Garlic Pita Chips, 31
 Garlic Toasts, 31
 Whole Roasted Garlic, 55
Gravlax, 126
Grilled Corn and Chile Salsa, 59
Grilled Eggplant Dip, 17
Grilled Quesadilla, 62
Grilled Yellow Peppers with Salsa Verde, 46
Guacamole with a Kick, 26
Ham Mousse in Cucumber Cups, 106
Herbed Clams in White Wine, 134
Herbed Olives, 52
Herbed Yogurt Cheese Dip, 13
Hummus, 24
Insalata Di Frutti Di Mare, 49
Jicama with Chili Dip, 67
Korean Barbecued Meatballs, 70
Light Guacamole, 61
Lobster Salad, Shrimp and, 124

M-R

Mascarpone-Stuffed Figs, 135
Meatballs
 Korean Barbecued Meatballs, 70
 Mexican Meatballs, 98
 Swedish Meatballs, 100

Microwave Cheese-Chorizo Dip, 65
Mini Puffs with Goat Cheese and Herbs, 115
Moroccan Triangles, 88
Mushroom Tartlets, 86
Mushrooms, Savory Stuffed, 104
Mussels and Mango, 121
Mustard Stuffed Eggs, 108
Nachos, No-Guilt, 69
Olive Paste Crostini, 34
Olives, Herbed, 52
Onion Rings, Classic, 76
Oriental Shrimp Platter, 120
Oven-Baked Tortilla Chips, 31
Oysters Rockefeller, 123
Pastries
  Cheese and Artichoke Crescents, 117
  Mini Puffs with Goat Cheese and Herbs, 115
  Moroccan Triangles, 88
  Pepper Jack Empanadas, 66
  Quiche Lorraine Squares, 85
  Samosas with Yogurt Sauce, 84
  Spinach Cheese Rolls, 114
Paté, Salmon, 110
Paté, Snapper, 107
Peanuts, Spicy Honey-Roasted, 81
Peppers
  Grilled Yellow Peppers with Salsa Verde, 46
  Red Pepper Chutney, 42
  Roasted Red Pepper Baguette, 39
Pesto Stuffed Eggs, 112
Pissaladiére, 37
Pizza, Smoked Salmon, 125
Pork
  Ham Mousse in Cucumber Cups, 106
  Mexican Meatballs, 98
  Microwave Cheese-Chorizo Dip, 65
  Spicy Pork Tenderloin with Lime Mayonnaise, 101
  Thai Dumplings, 138
  Zesty Bacon and Horseradish Dip, 71
Potato Latkes, 139
Potatoes with Sour Cream and Caviar, Roasted, 135
Potted Shrimp, 96
Quesadilla, Grilled, 62
Quesadillas, Yankee Grilled, 64
Quiche Lorraine Squares, 85
Ratatouille Salad, Quick, 50
Roasted Potatoes with Sour Cream and Caviar, 135

Roasted Red Pepper Baguette, 39
Roquefort-Walnut Dip, 16

S-Z
Salad
  Insalata Di Frutti Di Mare, 49
  Quick Ratatouille Salad, 50
  Shrimp and Lobster Salad, 124
  Smoked Trout Salad, 128
Salmon Paté, 110
Salmon Pizza, Smoked, 125
Salsa
  Black Bean Salsa, 58
  Classic Salsa Cruda, 29
  Crunchy Jicama Salsa, 21
  Fried Calamari with Creamy Salsa, 79
  Grilled Corn and Chile Salsa, 59
  Grilled Yellow Peppers with Salsa Verde, 46
  Salsa Verde, 30
Samosas with Yogurt Sauce, 84
Sandwiches, Shrimp Pinwheel, 95
Sandwiches, Smoked Salmon Ribbon, 93
Seafood
  Caviar Crown Mold, 96
  Crab Cakes with Two Sauces, 132
  Fresh Spring Rolls, 131
  Fried Calamari with Creamy Salsa, 79
  Gravlax, 126
  Herbed Clams in White Wine, 134
  Insalata Di Frutti Di Mare, 49
  Luscious Lime Shrimp, 91
  Mussels and Mango, 121
  Oriental Shrimp Platter, 120
  Oysters Rockefeller, 123
  Potted Shrimp, 96
  Roasted Potatoes with Sour Cream and Caviar, 135
  Salmon Paté, 110
  Shrimp and Lobster Salad, 124
  Shrimp Pinwheel Sandwiches, 95
  Shrimp Toasts with Soy Dipping Sauce, 94
  Smoked Salmon Pizza, 125
  Smoked Salmon Ribbon Sandwiches, 93
  Smoked Trout Salad, 128
  Snapper Paté, 107
  Tex-Mex Grilled Scampi, 129
  Thai Dumplings, 138
Sesame-White Bean Dip, 25

Shrimp and Lobster Salad, 124
Shrimp Pinwheel Sandwiches, 95
Skordalia, 19
Smoked Salmon Pizza, 125
Smoked Salmon Ribbon Sandwiches, 93
Smoked Trout Salad, 128
Snapper Paté, 107
Southwest Taco Dip, 60
Spicy Honey-Roasted Peanuts, 81
Spicy Pork Tenderloin with Lime Mayonnaise, 101
Spinach Cheese Rolls, 114
Spinach Dip, Fresh, 9
Spring Rolls, Fresh, 131
Stuffed Mushrooms, Savory, 104
Swedish Meatballs, 100
Sweet and Sassy Cashews, 80
Taco Dip, Southwest, 60
Taramasalata, 18
Tex-Mex Grilled Scampi, 129
Thai Dumplings, 138
Timing is Everything, 105
Tomato Jam, Double, 14
Tomato Bruschetta, 43
Tuscan Beans, 54
Whole Roasted Garlic, 55
Wine Biscuits, 75
Yankee Grilled Quesadillas, 64
Zesty Bacon and Horseradish Dip, 71
Zucchini Fritters with Coriander Chutney, 90
Zucchini Ribbons, 141

Tips
Crudités with Class, 9
Cleaning Shrimp, 91
Cool It, 103
Flower Ice Bucket, 139
How Much to Serve?, 97
Say it with Cheese, 54
Stocking the Bar, 108
The Antipasto Pantry, 42
The Way to Deep Fry, 76
Timing is Everything, 105
Veggies That Take the Plunge, 23

METRIC COOKING HINTS

By making a few conversions, cooks in Australia, Canada, and the United Kingdom can use the recipes in Ladies' Home Journal® *100 Great Appetizer and Snack Recipes* with confidence. The charts on this page provide a guide for converting measurements from the U.S. customary system, which is used throughout this book, to the imperial and metric systems. There also is a conversion table for oven temperatures to accommodate the differences in oven calibrations.

Volume and Weight: Americans traditionally use cup measures for liquid and solid ingredients. The chart (top right) shows the approximate imperial and metric equivalents. If you are accustomed to weighing solid ingredients, here are some helpful approximate equivalents.
- 1 cup butter, caster sugar, or rice = 8 ounces = about 250 grams
- 1 cup flour = 4 ounces = about 125 grams
- 1 cup icing sugar = 5 ounces = about 150 grams

Spoon measures are used for smaller amounts of ingredients. Although the size of the tablespoon varies slightly among countries, for practical purposes and for recipes in this book, a straight substitution is all that's necessary.

Measurements made using cups or spoons should always be level, unless stated otherwise.

Product Differences: Most of the ingredients called for in the recipes in this book are available in English-speaking countries. However, some are known by different names. Here are some common American ingredients and their possible counterparts:
- Sugar is granulated or caster sugar.
- Confectioners' sugar is icing sugar.
- All-purpose flour is plain household flour or white flour. When self-rising flour is used in place of all-purpose flour in a recipe that calls for leavening, omit the leavening agent (baking soda or baking powder) and salt.
- Light corn syrup is golden syrup.
- Cornstarch is corn flour.
- Baking soda is bicarbonate of soda.
- Vanilla is vanilla essence.
- Green, red or yellow sweet peppers are capsicums.
- Sultanas are golden raisins.

USEFUL EQUIVALENTS: U.S. = AUST./BR.

⅛ teaspoon = 0.5 ml
¼ teaspoon = 1 ml
½ teaspoon = 2 ml
1 teaspoon = 5 ml
1 tablespoon = 1 tablespoon
¼ cup = 2 tablespoons = 2 fluid ounces = 60 ml
⅓ cup = ¼ cup = 3 fluid ounces = 90 ml
½ cup = ⅓ cup = 4 fluid ounces = 120 ml
⅔ cup = ½ cup = 5 fluid ounces = 150 ml
¾ cup = ⅔ cup = 6 fluid ounces = 180 ml
1 cup = ¾ cup = 8 fluid ounces = 240 ml
1¼ cups = 1 cup
2 cups = 1 pint
1 quart = 1 litre
½ inch = 1.27 centimetres
1 inch = 2.54 centimetres

BAKING PAN SIZES

American	Metric
8x1½-inch round baking pan	20x4-centimetre cake tin
9x1½-inch round baking pan	23x3.5-centimetre cake tin
11x7x1½-inch baking pan	28x18x4-centimetre baking pan
13x9x2-inch baking pan	30x20x3-centimetre baking pan
2-quart rectangular baking dish	30x20x3-centimetre baking pan
15x10x2-inch baking pan	38x25.5x2-centimetre baking pan (Swiss roll tin)
9-inch pie plate	22x4- or 23x4-centimetre pie plate
7- or 8-inch springform pan	18- or 20-centimetre springform or loose-bottom cake tin
9x5x3-inch loaf pan	23x13x7-centimetre or 2-pound narrow loaf tin or paté tin
1½-quart casserole	1.5-litre casserole
2-quart casserole	2-litre casserole

OVEN TEMPERATURE EQUIVALENTS

Fahrenheit Setting	Celsius Setting*	Gas Setting
300°F	150°C	Gas Mark 2
325°F	160°C	Gas Mark 3 (moderately slow)
350°F	180°C	Gas Mark 4 (moderate)
375°F	190°C	Gas Mark 5 (moderately hot)
400°F	200°C	Gas Mark 6 (hot)
425°F	220°C	Gas Mark 7
450°F	230°C	Gas Mark 8 (very hot)
Broil		Grill

Electric and gas ovens may be calibrated using Celsius. However, increase the Celsius setting 10 to 20 degrees when cooking above 160°C with an electric oven. For convection or forced-air ovens (gas or electric), lower the temperature setting 10°C when cooking at all heat levels.